STREETS
OF
DOVER

by Derek Leach OBE

Riverdale Publications 24 Riverdale, River, Dover, CT17 0QX

Sir Walter Raleigh reported these words of Thomas Digges to Elizabeth I: *"No promontory, town or haven in Christendom is so placed by nature and situation, both to gratify friends and annoy enemies as this town of Dover; no place is so settled to receive and deliver intelligence for all matters and actions in Europe, from time to time; no town is by nature so settled ... to train inhabitants by land to make it great, fair, rich and populous ... nor is there any port... more convenient, needful or rather of necessity to be regarded than this of Dover"*.

Published in 2009 by Riverdale Publications
24 Riverdale, River, Dover CT17 0QX

ISBN 978-0-9536166-8-8

Printed in England by A. R. Adams (Printers) Ltd.,
The Printing House, Dour Street, Dover CT16 1EW

Contents

PART 1

The Growth of Dover town

PART 2

PLAN

OF

DOVER

(PIKE'S BLUE BOOK SERIES)

Introduction

Situated at the mouth of the River Dour, a small chalk stream flowing into the English Channel, Dover always was, and still is, strategically placed at the shortest crossing point to continental Europe. Over the centuries from at least Roman times the river was crucial to Dover's existence, providing a sheltered haven for shipping and a constant source of fresh water as well as power for a variety of industries. The original estuary that the Romans knew became choked with silt and shingle and much of modern Dover is built over the ancient haven. Defended by a succession of Iron Age, Roman, medieval, Napoleonic and later fortifications, the most impressive of them – the extensive medieval castle – still dominates the town from its lofty perch.

Dover fits into the general pattern of town development albeit with its unique geographical position so close to continental Europe. The Romans introduced an urban society and culture to Britain, which declined rapidly after their departure, but the 9th and 10th centuries saw a revival when mints and markets began to play key roles. By 1086 10% of the population is thought to have lived in towns, remaining more or less static for some 500 years. Towns often acquired town walls in medieval times within which were closely set houses fronting directly onto streets. Once population numbers recovered after the Black Death, the 16th century was a time of declining trade with much vagrancy and poverty. From this time on most towns grew continuously either primarily as manufacturing centres, as ports or later as pleasure resorts – some managing to combine all three elements. Overcrowding and problems of urban living were gradually overcome by the 19th and 20th century reform of local government and by improvements to sanitation (both water supply and sewage disposal) as well as by slum clearance and rehousing.

Dover is steeped in history, but this book concentrates upon its physical growth and development from earliest times to the present day. It also provides an extensive list of past and present streets in the current Dover Town Council area with information, wherever possible, about their formation (and, where appropriate, their demolition) and an explanation for the name of the road. I cannot guarantee the accuracy of all the street information gathered from a number of official and unofficial sources which, on occasion, have conflicted with each other and which I have been unable to verify. If any reader has incontrovertible evidence about any of the dubious claims, I should be pleased to receive them.

Derek Leach

PART 1

Chapter 1
Up to 1066

The River Dour rises just seven miles inland before flowing into the sea at what the Romans called Dubris, the Saxons called Dwyffra and we now call Dover. With the Dour valley being the only break in the line of the White Cliffs, from time immemorial a haven at Dover has been important for trade with the continent only 20 miles across the Channel, as a base for ships to defend the country from attack and for kings and princes journeying to the continent to make war, to negotiate peace or to seek a bride. The first recorded description of Dover and its bay was by Julius Caesar in 55BC when he tried to land, 'The sea was confined by mountains so close to it that a dart could be thrown from their summit upon the shore.'

The valley between the high white cliffs was settled long before the Roman invasion in 43 AD and the exciting discovery by workmen of the Bronze Age Boat in 1992, buried six metres below the streets of Dover, indicates that sea-going craft were crossing the Channel and putting into this haven about 3,600 years ago. Other evidence has been found of people living in the area around 2000BC. The Dour estuary was a valuable haven for the Romans, evidenced by the remains discovered by archaeologists in 1855 and in the 1950s of the harbour constructed close to the present Market Square. It may have stretched from the present King Street to Russell Street and inland beyond the present Castle Street. The demolition of war-damaged buildings after the Second World War gave archaeologists opportunities to discover the extent of the Roman settlement with several finds in the town centre in the 1940s and 50s, but 1970 saw the start of an extensive excavation programme prior to the construction of the York Street dual carriageway and the redevelopment of part of the town centre. Fifty major structures of varying periods were found, including fine Roman buildings, the best of which is the superb Roman Painted

Bronze Age Boat

Roman Fort

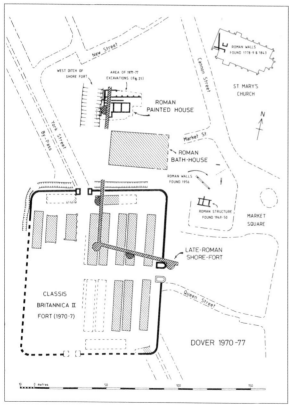

Diagram of Roman Dover (KARU)

House, which can be viewed today off New Street. One of the most complete Roman forts ever found in southern Britain was also unearthed. Spread over two acres, it proved to be the base for the Roman British fleet, taking advantage of the safe haven. In addition substantial remains of a later fort, the Saxon shore fort, built by the Roman army after the naval fort had been abandoned, were found. This was needed to combat the ever increasing Saxon raids at the end of the third century. A substantial portion of a Roman military bathhouse was also found. On the cliffs on both sides of the valley the Romans built lighthouses to guide their ships into port, one of which, the Pharos, can still be seen today alongside the church of St. Mary in Castro – said to be one of the finest surviving Roman monuments in western Europe, the highest Roman structure in Britain and one of only three surviving Roman lighthouses. No doubt the settlement at Dover prospered from increased trade with the Roman Empire. Proof of its importance is the Roman road from Dover to London and another from Dover to Richborough, which was another important Roman base.

The Roman occupation of Britain ended early in the fifth century and was followed by invasions by the Jutes, the Saxons and the Danes. There is archaeological evidence of an Anglo-Saxon settlement by the start of the 6th century within the walls of the late Roman shore fort. The arrival of St. Augustine in 597 and the subsequent conversion of King Ethelbert of Kent to

Roman Pharos

Christianity led to an increase in cross Channel trade and, together with herring fishing, the town prospered and grew. The site of the Anglo-Saxon harbour is not known, but any surviving Roman harbour east of the shore fort was possibly still useable. It is known that royal fleets used Dover as a base in 1036, 1051 and 1066.

Religious buildings
The large number of churches and religious houses are an indication of the size and importance of the town at this time.

St. Martin Le Grand
The first substantial building constructed in Dover after Roman times was probably the priory of St. Martin Le Grand. According to Statham, in his History of Dover published in 1899, the monastery was founded during the reign of King Withred of Kent (691 to 725AD) when he removed the 22 secular canons from the castle area. The Saxon structure was rebuilt by the Normans, following their policy of replacing Saxon buildings. It was cruciform in shape and possibly 220 feet long with considerable quantities of recycled Roman materials used in the construction. Following the foundation of the new

St. Martin Le Grand

3

priory of St. Martin the Newark (i.e. new work) in 1131 (the site is now Dover College), St. Martin Le Grand became a parish church with all its lands and possessions transferred to the new foundation. Strangely, the parish altars of St. Nicholas and St. John were set up in the church probably before the late 13th century.

St. Mary in Castro

Adjacent to the Roman lighthouse on the eastern heights stands the church of St. Mary in Castro. Despite

St. Mary in Castro prior to Victorian restoration

the large scale restoration in the 19th century it remains the finest late Saxon building in Kent, dating from the late 10th or early 11th century. This church may have formed part of an Anglo-Saxon fortified settlement and its original grandeur indicates a possible royal or noble base. Evidence of many Saxon burials close by indicate a pre-Conquest civilian settlement here, suggesting both upper and lower Dover settlements.

St. Mary the Virgin in 1805

St. Mary the Virgin

The church of St. Mary the Virgin in Cannon Street may also date from Saxon times, being one of the three religious buildings erected by the secular canons of St. Martin Le Grand. It was rebuilt by the Normans and we now know that it was built on part of the site of a Roman bath house. The church was controlled by the secular canons until after the Norman Conquest, but was given to the Maison Dieu in the reign of King John. At the Dissolution it was saved from demolition when the town petitioned Henry VIII to grant it for use as a parish church. It thus became the civic church and from 1585 until the 19th century the mayor was elected there. Unfortunately, because of its weak foundations, the church, except for the magnificent tower, was rebuilt in 1842-43, although some of its Norman arches and columns were reinstated.

Old St. James's Church

St. James's Church and parish

St. James's Church, at the end of St. James's Street, is mentioned in the Domesday Monachorium, suggesting a pre-Norman Conquest origin, but the Norman structure dates from the 12th century. Following the building of New St. James' Church in 1862, the old church became a chapel of ease. Badly damaged during the Second World War, it was not demolished but was retained as a tidy ruin. It was built to cater for the settlement that developed between the castle and the River Dour and its parish extended from the west bank of the river to the castle walls and from the sea shore to the Charlton parish boundary. Evidence of this early settlement was found in 1996, during excavations in Townwall Street prior to redevelopment of a petrol filling station. Dating from the later 12th century were a series of small building plots with timber dwellings on both sides of what became Clarence Street. On this site a significant amount of fish bone, fish hooks and other fishing equipment were found, indicating occupation by poorer folk and underlining the importance of fishing to this area. From 1550 onwards stone buildings appeared, but the south side was cleared eventually to build Clarence House, which was itself demolished to make way for the Burlington Hotel. St. James's Street was the main street of the parish, following the line of a shingle ridge with Clarence Street running almost parallel to seaward and Dolphin Lane to landward. The much later Trevanion and Woolcomber streets may have had their origins in tracks from the beach made by wagons and pack animals on their way to the castle with building stone and other materials landed on the beach. Upmarket was a local market serving the parish and the castle.

St. Peter's Church

The church of St. Peter was probably built by the secular canons of St. Martin Le Grand and was used as the civic church where the mayor was elected from at least 1367 until 1581. Elizabeth I granted it to the Corporation to be sold with the money to be spent improving the harbour. Thomas Allyn, the mayor, however, seems to have disappeared with the money! The parish became part of St. Mary's parish in 1611. The church was gradually demolished and replaced with homes and businesses. The *City of Antwerp Inn* occupied the site on one side of the Market Square until the Lloyds Bank building replaced it in 1905.

Raiders

Dover suffered from Danish raiders from the end of the eighth century, which culminated in their invasion of Kent in 994. By the mid 10th century the town possessed a mint, evidence of a sizeable community, and by 1066 some sort of guildhall where commercial transactions were conducted. There were three separate areas of settlement: around St. Martin Le Grand, at the foot of Warden Down (Castle Hill) and around St. Mary in Castro within the earth and timber Saxon defences.

Domesday Book

The Domesday Book of 1086, commissioned by William the Conqueror, valued the town at £40, which suggests that there was not only a rapid recovery from the burning of the town by William's troops in 1066 but an expansion, since it was double the value recorded during Edward the Confessor's reign, 1042-1066. Domesday also tells us something about Dover during the reign of Edward the Confessor, the last Saxon king of England. The town was required to provide the monarch, free of charge for 15 days a year, 20 ships each crewed by 15 men and a boy. In return the king granted Dover several important privileges: permission to raise its own taxes, the right to try all civil and criminal cases in its own courts (sac), power to compel all those living within its jurisdiction to plead in its courts (soc) and the right to make a fixed charge for the king's messengers when crossing the Channel. It is likely that these privileges were granted long before Edward the Confessor, possibly by Alfred the Great, as a means to provide a navy against the Danes. Similar privileges in exchange for ship service were extended to the other Cinque Ports of Sandwich, Hythe, Romney and Hastings. In peacetime these ships were used for fishing or transporting goods and passengers across the Channel, but in times of war transported the king's armies to the continent or were converted into fighting vessels, being used not only in the Channel but wherever needed around the coast of Britain. These actions sometimes decimated the Dover fishing fleet and affected the general prosperity of the town until new ships were built on the beach. There were possibly 400 townsmen in 1086.

The importance of sea fishing is illustrated by a reference in Domesday Book to the imposition of the king's truce, enforced by the king's reeve, from 29 September to 30 November. This period was the North Sea herring fishing season when many of the town's boats and leading citizens would have been absent, making policing the town difficult without strong royal authority.

Whilst the short herring season was lucrative, the townsmen, when not involved with the king's ship service or working the passage, would turn their hands to anything to make a living: boat building and repairs, farming smallholdings and piracy!

We may conclude that at the time of the Norman Conquest in 1066 Dover was of considerable importance, having valuable municipal privileges, defended by a strong fortress on the eastern heights, although not of stone, being the official means of communication with the continent and boasting a large monastic foundation. After defeating Harold at Senlac at the Battle of Hastings, realising its strategic importance, William made his way to Dover and took the castle. Unfortunately, his troops, no doubt elated by their success, burnt the town. The 16th century historian, Lambarde, states that only 29 houses were left standing. Apparently this was not ordered by William since he punished the soldiers and compensated the townspeople. With peace restored, Dover prospered once again from its herring fishing and 'working the passage' as the cross Channel trade was known, which increased substantially after the Conquest with both the king and his nobles owning land on both sides of the Channel.

Chapter 2
From 1066 to 1600

Medieval Dover comprised the military quarter on Castle Hill, the fishermen's quarter under Castle Cliff, the ecclesiastical quarter around St. Martin Le Grand and the commercial quarter around Queen Street. The main focus continued to be the former Roman area on the south west side of the valley below the Western Heights. The constant silting of the river mouth was a problem and possibly in the 1100s it silted up completely, causing the Dour to divide at what we now know as Stembrook with the Eastbrook flowing below Castle Cliff into Dover Bay and the Westbrook flowing into the bay toward Archcliffe. Ships may then have used the shelter of Castle Cliff close to (old) St. James' Church. This whole theory, however, is now in doubt as the result of recent archaeological findings.

Archaeological excavations in the area bounded by the modern Townwall Street, Woolcomber Street, Castle Street and Bench Street have revealed evidence of low status timber buildings, dating from the 12th and 13th centuries, which indicates that this area was intensively occupied at this time with the open beach used for landing fish, drying nets and beaching boats. The earliest development in this area appeared to be along the line of St. James' Street followed by the old Townwall Street with the latter having up to 10 successive buildings on the same site with replacements every 10 or 20 years, sometimes due to fire.

Dover Castle
The view from the town was transformed between 1180 and 1275 when the magnificent stone castle was built on the orders of Henry II and completed by Henry III. This major and lengthy

Impression of Dover Castle c1300 by J.D. Flavin

construction project would have attracted numerous craftsmen and labourers to the town, providing a ready market for local fish, meat, bread, beer and other goods. Maurice the Engineer designed both the massive keep, built in 1180, and its double ring of defensive walls, the first of its kind in Europe. Strangely, whilst the concentric walls were the latest in military design, the impressive keep with 20 foot thick walls in places was traditional and outdated when built. It was multi-purpose, acting as a great storeroom, the occasional residence of the monarch and the royal court as well as the ultimate stronghold during a siege. It was soon put to the test for in 1216 the French occupied the town, took hostages and besieged the castle. This landmark with some modifications retained its military role until the 20th century before becoming a major tourist attraction.

Maison Dieu

The Maison Dieu was founded outside the town by Hubert de Burgh in 1203 as a free resting place for pilgrims travelling to and from the continent, many of them visiting the shrine of Thomas Becket at Canterbury. Later, destitute and wounded soldiers returning from continental wars were taken in as well as some permanent pensioners – people of note and not necessarily local – sometimes nominated by the king. Initially the building was only a large hall with kitchen and accommodation for the master and his staff. A chapel was added in 1227 and other buildings followed. When it was suppressed in 1536 as part of Henry VIII's Dissolution programme, buildings included a chapel, vestry, great chamber, small chamber, a chamber over the river, master's chamber, kitchen, stables, hospital, a granary, brewhouse, bakery and several barns. Livestock included 1600 sheep, 119 bullocks and 33 horses. The

Maison Dieu

8

foundation possessed lands around the county and in Dover owned lands from the present Ladywell to Dieu Stone Lane. The Crown turned the buildings and immediate area into a naval victualling yard and in the 19th century it was taken over by the Royal Engineers, together with Maison Dieu House, built in 1665 as the residence for the naval victualling yard manager. No longer needed by the Crown, the Maison Dieu was purchased by the Corporation in 1834 and a town gaol was built on the site of the Maison Dieu church beside the Stone Hall and used until 1868. The Stone Hall was beautifully restored between 1852 and 1862 and the former chapel became the council chamber in 1868. With gaols no longer a corporation responsibility the prison was demolished and the Connaught Hall was built on the site and opened in 1883.

St. Edmund's Chapel

St. Edmund's Chapel

The monks of the Maison Dieu provided Christian burials for the poor of the town and for sick pilgrims who did not reach Canterbury. St. Edmund's Chapel, which still stands today in Priory Road, was built by the monks in what was probably their burial ground and was consecrated in 1253 by St. Richard of Chichester.

Priory of St. Martin

It was in 1130, during Henry I's reign, that a new priory and church was consecrated and then built outside the town called St. Mary and St. Martin Newark (new work), using the revenue of St. Martin Le Grand. It consisted of a large cruciform church, a chapter house, dormitory, library, buttery, refectory, cloisters, gateway and king's hall, which was often used by the monarch when passing through Dover. During the French raid of 1295 St. Martin's Priory, as it was commonly known, was fired and ransacked. All the monks fled except one very old monk, Thomas De La Hale, who refused to reveal where the treasures of the priory were kept and was killed. In 1160

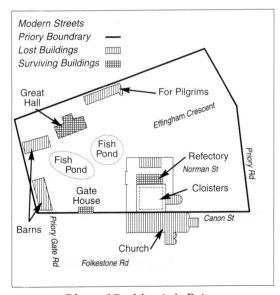

Plan of St. Martin's Priory

Priory Farm painted by William Burgess

Priory refectory when part of farm

Henry II granted the priory an eight day annual November fair, which lasted until the Dissolution in 1535 when the Corporation continued it near the ruins of St. Martin Le Grand in the area that became the Market Place. When gathering evidence for the Dissolution Henry VIII's Commissioners reported, 'The Prior of Dover and his monks are as bad as others. Sodomites there are none for they have no lack of women.' It was surrendered in 1540. The buildings and grounds were leased by the Archbishop of Canterbury for farming and most of the buildings were demolished or fell into disrepair. Fortunately, the grand Norman refectory was used as a barn and survives today. Dover College opened on the site in 1871 when the refectory and the gateway were restored and the king's hall became the college chapel.

St. Bartholomew's Hospital
Another religious foundation outside the town was St. Bartholomew's Hospital, dating from 1141, and built on what we know as Chapel Hill, Buckland. Its lands extended down the slope to the river. Catering for poor pilgrims initially, it soon became a leper hospital as well. Following suppression by Henry VIII in 1539, its buildings and lands were granted to John Bowle, Mayor of Dover, who demolished all the buildings.

Knights Templar Church
On the Western Heights there was another Norman church of which little is known, but thought to belong to the Knights' Templar. The remains, comprising a circular nave and walls four feet thick, were discovered in 1806 and can still be seen.

Archcliffe Chapel
Not much is known about Archcliffe Chapel, Our Lady of Pity. Since it was apparently already old when restored in 1530, when first built it must have been very remote, perhaps serving a few fishermen. Lyon states that it became a fisherman's home until 1576 when it was destroyed by rough seas.

Town walls
There has been much controversy about when Dover's town walls were constructed, but recent research by Dr. Sheila Sweetenburgh has shed new light on the subject by studying documents from Dover's various religious institutions, chamberlains' accounts and the calendars of royal records coupled with the results of recent archaeological excavations by Canterbury Archaeological Trust in the Townwall Street and Pier District areas.

Unlike many medieval towns where the defences of castle and town were integrated, those of Dover were completely separate from its castle. Whilst from 1180 Henry II and his successors built the massive keep and curtain wall of the castle, Dover appears to have been undefended.

Evidence of walled towns come primarily from the crown providing murage grants (mur being French for wall), the first being recorded in 1220. These gave towns the right to levy a toll for use in constructing and maintaining town walls on goods entering the town. Previously this cost fell upon the townspeople. In the 14th century there was a toll of 1d on each horseman, his horse and groom, whilst every merchant ship putting into Dover had to pay 4d or 6d. Some towns, however, may have used other methods to finance their walls and

Dover was probably one of them. Surviving charters contain references to the town wall that predate the Dover's first murage grant in 1324, the first reference being in 1231 followed by others in the 13th century. These indicate at least two sections of wall: one across at least part of the river mouth and the second an extension inland on the western side of the town.

The Corporation's normal expenditure was restricted to ceremonies, journeys (such as sending two burgesses to parliament for ten days costing 100 shillings), personal expenses, administering justice and defending the town. Any real work such as shifting shingle from the harbour's mouth or scouring the river bed was done without payment by freemen as a public duty. There were no 'council rates' as such. Income came from fines, rents from properties and maletots i.e. taxes on trade such as firewood, brewers and meat sellers. Fines included 3s 4d for having pigs in the road, 40s for striking with a sword and for using a knife 6s 8d. There was also income from the limbs of Dover as a Cinque Port since they had to pay Dover for the privilege.

Sources of necessary additional income for the walls included a tax of 12d a foot for new wall construction and 6d a foot for old wall repairs for those with property along the line of the town wall as well as part of the income from maletots. At one time half the royal tax on the passage to Calais was also allocated to Dover's walls.

The town wall probably extended furthest in the 15th century, but may not have completely encircled the town. The wall on the seaward side was probably two to three metres thick. Leland, writing in the 1530s, noted a strong wall on the sea side, but the rest partly fallen

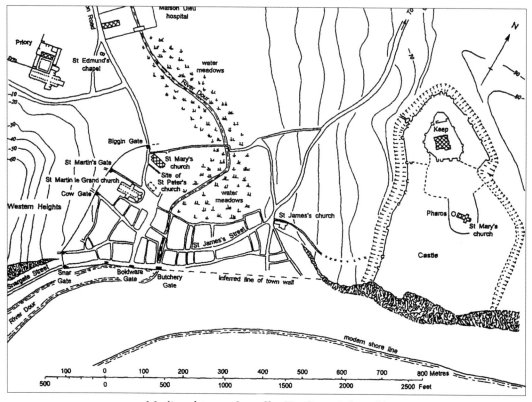

Medieval town & walls (Dr Sweetinburgh)

Butchery Gate / Hole in the Wall

down. Whilst recording gates on the seaward and western side, there is no mention of gates on the eastern flank, either because this section had disappeared or had never been built despite murage grants of 1406 and 1412 being 'for the enclosure of the town'. These town defences were augmented by several great guns.

A map of 1541 appears to show the following gates from the foot of Castle Cliff: Wardes (or Eastbrook) Gate, Cross (or St. Helen's) Gate and Segate (or Fisher's Gate), Butchery Gate (or Standfast Tower) spanned the river, Boldware Gate (sometimes called Severus Gate and demolished 1762) and Snar Gate (demolished 1683). With the watchtower at Archcliffe these gates and the connecting wall comprised the seaward defences in the Middle Ages. The western gates, probably Walgate (called Adrian's Gate by Lyon in his history of Dover) and Cow Gate (demolished 1776), were probably smaller and less impressive than the others, but Biggin Gate (demolished 1762) on the northern side of the town was probably substantial, providing the access to and from Canterbury and London.

Whilst defence against both the sea and foreign raiders was the primary reason for the walls – French raids on the town were a feature of the 13th century, including 1295 when the French raided with some 300 ships and 5,000 men – they also acted as visual boundaries of the town's jurisdiction even when the town extended beyond its walls. The wall gates, being entry points, were convenient for collecting tolls and, at night, closing of the gates kept out undesirables. These same walls also served to reinforce the authority and prestige of the mayor and jurats when surrounded on the one hand by the walled castle, demonstrating the mighty power of the king, and on the other by the walled religious institutions of St. Martin's Priory and the Maison Dieu, emphasising the power of the church.

The cost of maintaining the walls was heavy until the late 15th century and by the end of the century the town was fighting a losing battle with the sea and its walls were in a ruinous state, although Eldred's map of 1641 shows walls surviving from Snar Gate to Biggin Gate.

The network of streets inside the walled area, however, largely survived until the early 20th century.

Snargate Street

Snargate Street originally ran from Bench Street to little more than the present York Street roundabout. Its first extension was probably around 1370 when Snar Gate was erected some 100 yards further along the shore. To the west of this the sea still washed the cliffs. As land was gradually reclaimed the street was extended further westwards.

Pilgrims and soldiers

A substantial part of the town area was occupied by religious buildings. Within the walls were St. Martin Le Grand, St. Mary's, St. Peter's and St. James's. Beyond the walls were the Maison Dieu, the Priory of St. Martin and St. Bartholomew's Hospital.

Dover profited from the enormous increase in the flow of pilgrims across the Channel, helped by Henry III's royal charter decreeing that all pilgrims must leave England via Dover or face imprisonment for a year, whilst the capture of Calais in 1347 provided Dover with a peaceful ten year monopoly of trade with that port. Tragedy, however, struck the town and the whole of England in 1348 when the Black Death decimated the population, affecting the growth of the town for some years. The main form of employment was what we would now call service industries rather than manufacture – transport, accommodation and food – reflecting the importance of the cross Channel traffic. This dependence upon 'working the passage' also made Dover's prosperity vulnerable to bad weather and the presence of hostile forces in the Channel. Townsfolk were also expected to bear the cost of food and lodging for troops awaiting ships for France. Outsiders who wanted to do business in the town paid an annual fee for the privilege.

Town wards

Dover was divided into many wards – electoral wards still exist today – and in 1429, according to Statham, they were called: Bekyn, Burman, Bullys, Canon, Castledene, Derman, Delfys, Deeper, Halfguden, Horsepol, Moryns, Nankyn, Ox, Snargate, Syngyl, St. Mary, St. George, St. Nicholas, Upmarket, Werston and Wolvys. In 1470 Bochery and Shipman wards are mentioned and later Hither and Lower parts of North and South Pier were added. Each ward had a representative whose duty was to ensure that watchmen did their duty and, at a time when most buildings were largely of timber, fire precautions were enforced; every householder was compelled to have a tub of water outside the door at night in case of fire. In addition each ward was licensed for one passenger vessel to carry people to Witsand, which was the usual cross Channel port until Calais was captured. This was to ensure that vessels were always ready to serve the king when required.

1500

By 1500 the town was spilling out over the 14th century walls with the beginnings of new residential areas to the north and east. The fields beyond the Biggin Gate were disappearing and the land between the old fishermen's quarters in Dolphin Lane and Warden Down was filling with houses as well as a brewery, stables and a tannery. Many of the town gates no longer worked and the old town walls had houses and shacks built up against them. Inland between Charlton and Buckland the river separated into several small streams, forming boggy areas where osiers grew and were harvested for basket making. St. Martin Le Grand was falling into decay and both St. James' and St. Peter's were in a poor condition. St. Martin's Priory and the Maison Dieu were shadows of their splendid pasts, whilst around them new domestic buildings were springing up. Henry VII's edict that English goods should be carried in English ships helped Dover's fleet to prosper, although seafarers were affected by the drop in demand for barrels of salted herrings and other fish as well as a dramatic decline in the number of pilgrims passing through the town.

Dissolution

The Fishmarket and the Pennyless Bench were used as market places until 1479 when a cross was set up in Cross Place, the present Market Square, for a common market to be held. This became the site of the town hall and shambles (meat market). Up until the Dissolution, 1536-1540, the town was contained within its walls with virtually nothing beyond Biggin Gate except the Maison Dieu, the Priory and St. Bartholomew's Hospital. The churches and religious houses of Dover were all affected to a lesser or greater extent by Henry VIII's Dissolution of the Monasteries. The Maison Dieu, the Priory and St. Bartholomew's Hospital were all suppressed. The main building of the Maison Dieu was saved from demolition since it was taken over by the Crown for use as a naval victualling yard. St. Mary's was saved by Henry granting it to the town for use as the civic church. By the end of the 16th century St. Peter's had been sold and demolished to raise funds for the repair of the harbour, the nave and aisles of St. Martin Le Grand had also been demolished and the materials reused for building elsewhere. The town gained possession of the buildings and the surrounding land and the nave area was used as a burial ground for St. Mary's. Much of the east end survived until 1881. What little remains today can be seen beside the Discovery Centre.

Queen's Storehouse

A document in the East Kent Archives entitled 'A view of the Queen's Storehouse called Maison Dieu in January 1590' provides a description of what the Maison Dieu probably comprised at the time of its dissolution; although, we need to bear in mind that in 1590 the buildings were being used as a victualling store for the navy and some buildings may

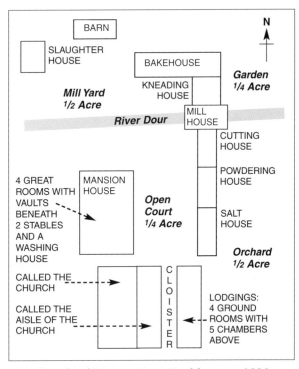

Sketch of Maison Dieu Buildings in 1590

have changed their uses. There was a mansion house with four good rooms and a vault underneath plus two stables, a washing house with bedchambers above. A gallery led to a lodging house with a cloister on the east side of the gallery. At the east end of the gallery was a building with four grand rooms and five bedchambers above. On the south side of the gallery was a very large building formerly part of the church, 108 feet by 27 feet, containing a ground room with two large bedchambers above. On the west side of the former church was a large room formerly an aisle, 110 feet by 45 feet, with a partial loft over, but with the roof partially collapsed and the rest decayed (i.e. the Stone Hall). At the east side of the courtyard were three rooms called the Cutting House, the Powdering House and the Salthouse in total 160 feet by 14 feet with a loft above. Beyond an orchard there was a Millhouse with two windmills, one for wheat and one for 'mault'. Adjacent was a Kneading House and then a Bakehouse, 100 feet by 39 feet, with three very large ovens plus a barn with five bays. Beyond the mill yard was a slaughterhouse. Surrounded by a stone wall was five acres of ground called Maison Dieu Park leased to a Mr. Skevington.

East Brook Water

By 1566 East Brook Water was formed. This was a tidal lagoon some 500 metres long and 100 metres wide enclosed by an extensive shingle spit as far as Castle Cliff. Construction of longer and longer piers to prevent shingle blocking the harbour mouth at the western end of the bay had caused shingle to be deposited across the bay. Whilst the western end of the lagoon, fed by the Dour, had been adapted, during Elizabeth I's reign, to store water, which

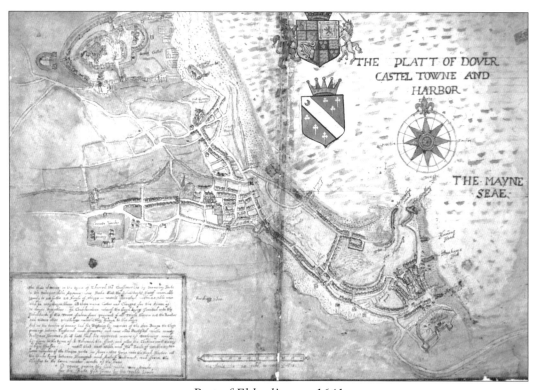

Part of Eldred's map 1641

16

was then released at intervals to scour the harbour mouth free of shingle, the narrower eastern end, denied fresh water, silted up. It is shown on Eldred's map of 1641 with a shingle bank seawards, but it was eventually filled in and a 1737 map shows the area occupied by garden plots, possibly market gardens. Eventually Liverpool Street was built across it in 1817. The present day shore line marks the outer beach ridge of the East Brook Water lagoon.

Depression

In 1565 Dover comprised 358 houses. The number would not have been much greater in 1649 when the town petitioned Cromwell regarding the state of the harbour and claimed that 200 houses in Dover were empty as a result. William Lambarde in his *Perambulation of Kent*, published in 1570, stated that the town with an estimated population of 2,000 had decayed, describing Dover as 'miserable nakedness and decay' due to the poor state of the harbour, the loss of the religious houses following the Dissolution and the loss of Calais in 1558, which was a severe blow for Dover's merchants. The town also had to cope with a flood of refugees. The Dover area suffered an earthquake in 1583, although no damage to the town is recorded, there were cliff falls and the seaward end of the castle's curtain wall fell. The damage can still be seen today.

Henry VIII's defences

A primitive defensive work built in 1370 at Archcliffe was replaced in 1539 when Henry VIII ordered the construction of a substantial bulwark on the site. This was one of three gun positions built to deter any French landings at Dover. Archcliffe Fort, albeit rebuilt, survives as does Mote's Bulwark on the side of Castle Cliff.

In 1595 the French burnt part of the town. At this time building was spreading along Snargate Street where once the sea washed the cliffs as far as what we now call Union Street. The town walls were in disrepair and were being robbed for building materials and the town had begun to expand northwards outside its walls with ribbon development beyond the Maison Dieu up to the present Tower Hamlets junction occupied by 'out dwellers' who were not Dover citizens and therefore not allowed to live within the town.

Watercolour of Archcliffe Fort

Administration of the town

All the residents of the town, including the poor, were known as the commanalty of the town, but this included 'incomers' from other places unless Dover people acted as sureties. About half the adult males of the town were freemen who had the right to trade in the town, run businesses, train apprentices and have first pick of the market goods! Freeman status was acquired by being the son of a freeman, by marrying a freeman's daughter or occasionally by buying a freemanship. Originally all freemen took part in electing the mayor. The

Mote's Bulwark

Common Council comprised 37 freemen who met monthly to discuss town business. From 1556 their powers increased and only they could elect the mayor. Above this council were the 12 jurats, who, with the mayor, were the ruling group of the town and also the magistrates.

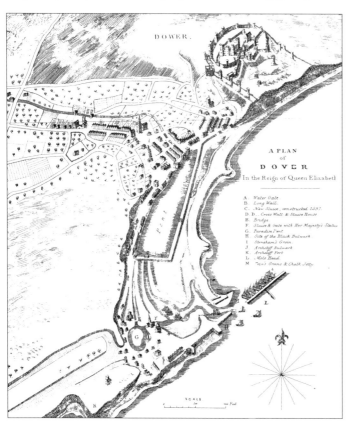

Plan of Town in Queen Elizabeth I's reign

From 1561 they held office for life! The mayor, however, was elected annually and was responsible for regulating the market, settling all minor offences and caring for widows and orphans. He also acted as coroner and was the contact between the town and the monarch and the Lord Warden. The four chamberlains were the town's treasurers who collected fines and taxes and also paid the corporation's bills, claiming back their money each year when they presented their accounts! There was also a bailiff, a Crown appointment, who was responsible for the town's prisons and for serious offenders not dealt with by the town court.

Chapter 3
1600 to 1800

Crime and punishment

Bunyer's (sometimes Bunger's) Bridge was built near the Pennyless Bench, which was rebuilt and enlarged (and not demolished until 1762). There were two prisons – one near the Bench for 'foreigners', meaning non freemen, and the other for freemen in a town wall tower called Standfast near Snar Gate. Near the fishmarket there was also a house of correction, commonly called 'the Hole', for those found guilty at quarter sessions courts. A new prison opened in 1613 for 'the better class of foreigner,' using the gate house of Biggin Gate. It was not until 1722 that the Hole or freemen's prison became the town jail for all offenders whether freemen or not and continued in use until 1746 when it was condemned as unfit and a new jail was built near the Market Square. The town had several alternative means of punishment, including the gallows, a pillory, a cage, stocks (removed in 1735) and a cucking stool as well as imposing whippings and cutting off ears.

Plague

A pest house existed in 1615 outside Cow Gate. This was not for anti-social behaviour, but to isolate poor people suffering from the plague or pestilence. This would have been totally insufficient to cope with the national outbreak of plague that afflicted Dover in 1665-66 when as many as 900 inhabitants may have died. The Corporation bought a piece of land on the side of the Western Heights overlooking the harbour where the dead were buried in plague pits; the site became known as The Graves.

Street cleaning

Householders were required to sweep clean the streets in front of their houses every Thursday. Bearing in mind that this could include the droppings of various animals it was as well that the town scavenger came around to collect the sweepings!

Revolution, plague and the state of the harbour all affected the prosperity and growth of the town, depending heavily as it did, and still does, on the success of the port.

Pier District

Dover's ships began to take shelter at the western end of the bay under Archcliffe when the old harbour silted up. A jetty was built in 1495 with two towers on it. This was such an improvement that the pool formed by the jetty was called Paradise. The little harbour, however, was constantly filled by shingle and eventually the sea won. Paradise Harbour became unusable and a new harbour was created between 1580 and 1600. By 1641 the area started to develop into a maze of narrow, crowded streets. A number of streets were built by 1737, including Snargate Street, Strond Street, Round Tower Street, Seven Star Street, Middle Row, Clarence Place, South Pier and Council House Street. The Crosswall, constructed in 1580 to enclose the Pent, was built upon in the 17th century and was called Snargate Street Over the Water or Snargate Street Over The Sluice; later it was renamed Union Street, probably after the *Union Hotel* on its corner. The old Paradise Pent, reduced to

Pier District c1835

Minet's Bank, demolished in 1873

a smelly marsh, was still not developed. By 1800, however, even this area, despite being low-lying and marshy, was in great demand for building. The Pier, as it was soon called locally, became a flourishing and important district with banks, hotels, stores, warehouses, pilots' houses and fishermen's cottages.

Apart from the Pier District, a 1737 plan of the town shows little change for more than a century with the town confined between the old York Street and Biggin Street, which by then was built up as far as the Maison Dieu. In 1728 the Market Place was enlarged by pulling down several houses.

Beach Street

Trade

By 1744 the practice of fining non-freemen 6s 8d a day for opening a shop was no longer enforced and by 1800 the two 'classes' of town dwellers, 'foreigner' and freeman, with the latter striving to keep all the trade in the town to themselves, had ended.

Trade at the port included exports of cod and herring, imports of coal from the North East, stone from the West Country and timber from Norway. There was also an important coastal trade with London, since little went by road: herrings, barley, malt, wool, paper, lime and kelp (seaweed used in the pottery and glass industry).

Travel

In 1555 parishes throughout the country were made responsible for repairing their roads by parishioners having to work on the roads for four days a year under the supervision of surveyors appointed by the churchwardens. These amateur efforts were quite ineffective and in the 17th century were replaced by cash payments. This sorry state of affairs was finally remedied by the building and maintenance of turnpike roads financed by tolls. In the early 18th century it could take three days to reach London from Dover by road, but the London to Dover road was still the most used in the country. Improvements to the main roads to and from Dover in the second half of the 18th century greatly increased traffic to the port and added to the prosperity of the town. The turnpike road to Canterbury and London opened in 1753, making use of London Road and the ford at Buckland before it was replaced by a bridge in 1800. In 1763 a turnpike road to Folkestone was built from Archcliffe Fort over the cliffs via Capel, but 20 years later the turnpike road was routed from the centre of Dover through Maxton, along what we now know as the Folkestone Road. Another turnpike road was established in 1796 to Sandwich via Deal, climbing Castle Hill via Laureston Place and what became the Zig Zag, although this was replaced in 1798 by a new road up the hill, which is the present Castle Hill. A few years later another opened through Waldershare and Eastry to Sandwich.

Buckland Bridge in 1800 by William Burgess

Mail coaches gradually took over the carrying of mail from the mounted post boys. The king's daily mail service from London to the continent via Dover had been instituted in 1660. In 1839 there were 13 coaching inns in the town, the most important being the *Royal Hotel*, the *Ship*, the *City of London*, the *King's Head* and the *York Hotel*. Steamships were introduced to the Channel crossing in 1820 improving sea journey times, but the land journey still relied upon coaches and horses.

In 1750

By 1750 the town walls had virtually disappeared, although the wall in Townwall Street was not demolished until 1818. The town council was meeting in its new Guildhall, built in 1605 in the Market Place. A market was held every Wednesday and Saturday plus an annual fair in November which lasted a fortnight. Much of the site of St. Martin Le Grand was in use as a

Guildhall and Market Place 1822

Phoenix Brewery in 1877

burial ground for St. Mary's and the Priory had become a farm. There was industrial development such as the Phoenix Brewery and Stembrook Tannery as well as the water-powered corn and paper mills along the Dour. The Pier District was developing fast and there were side roads off Biggin Street eastward toward the Dour.

Paving Commissioners

With Dover's streets in a bad state of repair, ill lit and filthy – householders deposited all sorts of household and human waste in the streets in addition to droppings from horses and other animals – parliament was petitioned for powers to better cleanse, light and watch the town. In 1778 the Dover Paving Act was passed. This provided for an annual tax of 6d in the pound on houses as well as a one shilling tax on every chaldron of coal arriving in Dover by land or sea to cover the cost of paving, cleaning, lighting and 'watching' the town. A separate Dover Paving Commission administered the arrangements, although it included the mayor and all the jurats (councillors), the two MPs, the Recorder, the Common Council plus 49 inhabitants, totalling 64. Quite a body! Initially it was only responsible for the parishes of St. Mary's and St. James, but later included Charlton and the town parts of Hougham parish.

The first street cleaning contract was awarded to Israel Claringbould; the annual payment for cleaning Dover's streets once a week was £10. The first paving contract, awarded in 1780, covered the road from the Victualling Office i.e. the Maison Dieu to King's Head Street in the Pier District. This was easier said than done because over the years householders had encroached upon the streets by building beyond their building line, usually 'bow windows' but sometimes even wash-houses! The powerful Paving Commissioners merely ordered the removal no matter how important the householder; although not everybody took it lying down! Mr. Christopher Gunman objected to demolition of a projecting window of his house in Biggin Street and obtained a High Court injunction to stop it; nevertheless, the Commissioners demolished it. Householders were ordered to fix gutters under the eaves with down pipes to ground level; if they had them already, they were instructed to clean them out. Removal of a number of dunghills was also ordered! Laying some drains proved very inconvenient since a few house 'necessaries' had to be demolished along the line of the drains. Fortunately, they were rebuilt at the Commissioners' expense! Many other streets were improved in quick succession.

King's Head pub that gave its name to the street

The Commissioners kept up the pressure upon householders and businesses with its Committee of Nuisances surveying streets regularly. An additional step was taken in 1786 when pigs, cows and bullocks were banned from pavements. Wheelbarrows and hobby horses soon followed suit. A King Street butcher was ordered to appear before the Commissioners for repeatedly killing pigs in the street.

In 1786 a night watch was instituted for the winter months, comprising seven watchmen who were provided with five watch boxes for shelter. Street safety was improved further with the provision in 1791 of 90 street lamps, later increased by another 37.

The Commissioners also took on the role of a planning authority with regard to new buildings or changes to buildings to ensure there was no encroachment into the street or interference with drains. Numbering of houses began in 1797.

Powers extended to the town's porters, who transported the baggage of cross Channel passengers from ship to hotel or stage coach and vice versa, because in 1814 rules, orders and charges were approved by the Commissioners.

Shop blinds projecting over the pavement were permitted in 1815 provided supports were at least seven feet from the ground.

In 1821 a radical decision was taken to install gas lights in the streets; although it took several years to implement. Surfacing the carriageway with tarmacadam also began in the 1820s. At this time the Commissioners ordered that 'soil' from privies should only be removed by the official night carts.

A Police Committee was formed in 1831 to oversee the creation of Dover's police force which took over the duties of the night watchmen in 1836.

The Paving Commission, which did so much to improve conditions in the town was dissolved in 1848 and its powers were transferred to the Dover Corporation.

Defensive works

In 1779 Britain was at war with America, France and Spain. This resulted in a flurry of defence works in and around the town. Four gun batteries each with 28 guns were built around the bay: North Battery in the centre, Guilford and Amherst to the east and Townshend

Grand Shaft Barracks

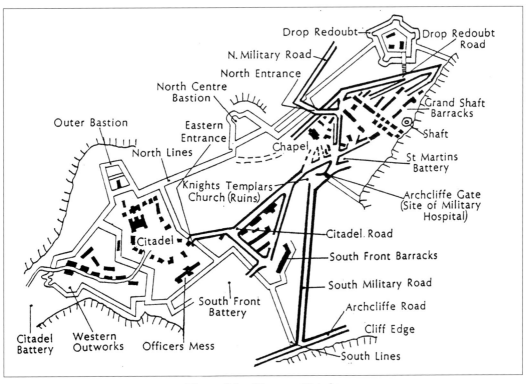

Plan of the Western Heights

to the west. These batteries were all demolished between 1830 and 1843. The first earthworks on the Western Heights were also constructed. The town's defences were also strengthened in 1806 by converting what was left of the East Brook into a military canal from Castle Cliff to New Bridge.

With the threat of invasion by Napoleon, elaborate defensive works on the Western Heights were begun, continuing until 1815 and the final defeat of Napoleon. The Grand Shaft Barracks and its incredible triple staircase were also built at this time. These defences were extended and strengthened in the 1860s when Emperor Napoleon III posed a similar threat. Finally abandoned in the 1960s with most of the barracks demolished and the Citadel used initially as a young offenders' institution and now as an Immigrant Removal Centre, these incredible defensive works in the care of English Heritage survive albeit mothballed. In any other town they would be a major attraction, but in Dover they are the poor relation of Dover Castle.

The castle was also strengthened and modified during this period (1794-99). Underground barracks in the cliff were constructed (reused and extended during the Second World War) to accommodate more troops, great earthworks and bastions were thrown up on the Deal side of the castle to thwart any landward attack, the keep was bomb-proofed, the curtain wall towers were modified to take modern guns on the roof and the medieval tunnels in the moat were modernised. Fort Burgoyne was begun in 1861 to protect the castle from a northern attack. Its casemated bomb-proof barracks were completed in 1868.

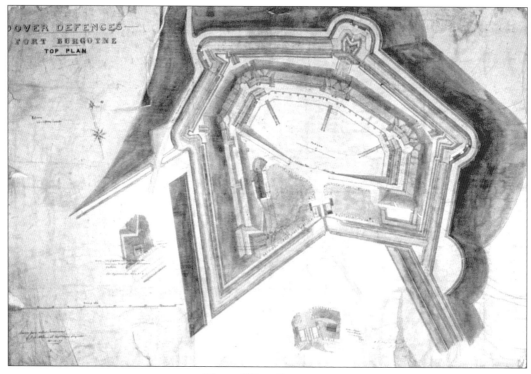

Plan of Fort Burgoyne

Chapter 4
1800 to 1900

Hasted in his *History of Kent* published in 1797 describes Dover thus, 'the town is at present exceeding wealthy and populous containing near 10,000 people'. This was probably a little exaggerated since in 1801 the population was officially 8,570 with fewer than 2,000 houses. In Baker's 1805 *Atlas of English Towns* Dover is described as 'a variety of neat and fashionable houses'. Was this the whole story or an attempt to lure visitors to the town? With suitable building land in short supply, dwellings had to be fitted into the available space between the cliffs and the sea. Snargate Street was the centre of economic activity and the Pier District, in addition to the general bustle offloading and unloading passengers and goods, contained the Post Office, the Custom House, inns, banks, warehouses, ship building and repair businesses.

In 1801 the Maison Dieu was still the limit of development up the valley. Charlton, Buckland and Dover were still separated by open country, but the villages also expanded greatly between 1801 and 1810: Buckland by 66%, Charlton by 115%, Hougham by 213% compared with the town parishes of St. Mary's and St. James' which increased by only 28%.

There were virtually no buildings on the cow pastures of the eastern slopes of the Western Heights pre 1800, but then Mr. Hartley built Prospect House followed by Portland Place, Hartley Street and Albany Place. Beginning in the late 1820s, the Durham Hill complex of streets, containing a warren of small working class dwellings, were constructed.

Prospect House

Hartley Street

Durham Hill

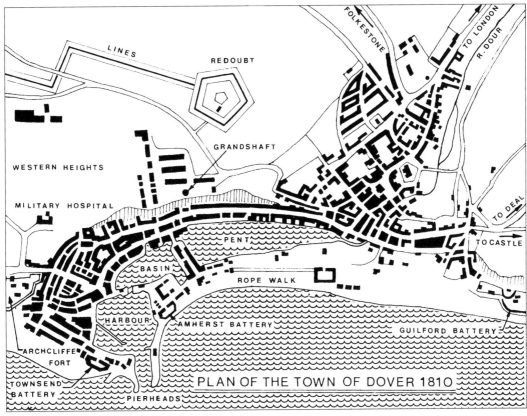

1810 Map

Boom conditions

The Napoleonic War years brought boom conditions to the town. In addition to the large garrison, possibly up to 10,000 men ready for any invasion, wealthy families used to touring Europe were confined to Britain by the war and took their holidays 'at home' including seaside holidays in Dover. This influx of visitors with time and money led to the construction of new theatres and assembly rooms with public breakfasts, card assemblies, banquets and balls. Bathing machines appeared as well as hot baths. A Wilkes and Barfoot publication stated that the town's 'delightful situation, purity of sea and the advantage of a fine beach' promised to make Dover 'one of the most fashionable watering places in the kingdom'. The population increased rapidly during the latter Napoleonic War years.

Post War

The peaceful period following the defeat of Napoleon in 1815 saw Dover develop as a seaside resort and this, with a substantial military garrison as well as the traditional port activities encouraged growth along the shoreline of the bay and up the valleys. By 1821 building had intensified in the vicinity of the harbour. The decayed Paradise Pent, disused for shipping since the late 16th century, was drained and built upon. Dover was connected to the villages of Buckland, Charlton and Hougham by ribbon development. Building had already begun on the shingle foreshore between the Pent and the beach and at the foot of Castle Cliff.

Rapid growth

Between 1821 and 1841 the population increased by 40%. The quick succession of local paving and lighting acts in 1778, 1810, 1830 and 1835, emphasise the rapid growth of the town. The last mentioned enabled the widening of Bench Street and the opening of Castle Street into the Market Place. The construction industry boomed with builders increasing from 4 to 23 and coal merchants from 3 to 12 in ten years.

Pigot's Dover Directory of 1839 describes 'warm and cold shower baths on the sea front, libraries and reading rooms with the best works'. William Cobbett in his *Rural Rides* pays Dover something of a backhanded compliment writing that there were 'less blackguard people in Dover than ever I observed in any seaport before'. By 1844 a continuous built up strip existed between the Western Heights and Castle Cliff, whilst both sides of Biggin Street were developed as far as the Maison Dieu.

The main growth of the town was along the line of the road to London and Canterbury, which followed the Dour. This ribbon development saw what were once separate villages absorbed into the town: Charlton, Buckland and part of Hougham in 1835. River was added in 1903 but regained parish council status in 1987. Extension of Dover along the Folkestone

Former Dover Union workhouse 1835

Beat 1 From the *Two Brewers* in Limekiln Street to Fort Hill, Bulwark Street, Hawkesbury Street, Oxenden Street as far as Old Post Office Lane, Round Tower Street, Crosswall and the whole of South Pier with intermediate streets, lanes, courts and alleys;

Beat 2 From Five Post Lane, down Snargate Street, Commercial Quay as far as Two Brewers Lane, Old Post Office Lane, Custom House Quay, Old Bank Lane, Strond Street and intermediate streets, lanes, courts and alleys;

Beat 3 From the Union Bridge, Union Street, past the *York Hotel* to the swing bridge, Amherst Battery, Esplanade, Waterloo Crescent, Camden Crescent and back to Union Bridge;

Camden Crescent

Waterloo Crescent

Last Lane

Beat 4 From the bottom of Marine Parade, Guilford Battery, Baltic Cottage, Liverpool Terrace, Hammond Place, Trevanion Street, Woolcomber Street, Townwall Street, Mill Lane, Fishmongers Lane and intermediate lanes, streets and alleys;

Beat 5 Bottom of Market Street, Market Lane, Queen Street, Chapel Lane, Five Post Lane, up to the top of Snargate Street, Bench Street, King Street, Market Place, Last Lane, Chapel Place, Adrian Street, Above Wall, with intermediate streets, lanes and alleys;

Beat 6 From Market Place, Stem-brook, Church Street, Castle Street, Eastbrook, St. James' Street, Hubert Terrace, Laureston Place, Dolphin Lane, Russell Street, with inter-mediate streets, lanes and alleys;

Beat 7 Market Street, Princes Street, Durham Hill, Mount Pleasant, Military Road, Worthington's Lane, lower part of Biggin Street, Cannon Street, with inter-mediate streets, lanes and alleys;

Woolcomber Street

Ladywell pre 1903

Peter Street

Beat 8 From Worthington's Lane, Biggin Street, Priory Street, Folkestone Road, through Priory Yard, High Street, Charlton Green, Peter Street, Bridge Street, Tower Hamlets, Ladywell, with intermediate streets, lanes, courts and alleys;

Beat 9 From Charlton Gate (*toll gate*), Buckland Street, Shooter's Hill, Pierce's Farm, Crabble Gate (*toll gate*) and Barton Farm.

All this was apparently accomplished by a force of 12 constables with only

Trevanion Street

three on night duty at any one time. Each had to report back to the Station House in Queen Street every two hours and meal breaks also had to be fitted in!

Oxenden Street

1844 map

Small's map of 1844 shows a built up area between the cliffs and the sea with the town centre something like a triangle narrowing as it reached the Maison Dieu with ribbon development up the London Road towards Buckland – little change from the previous 100 years except for infilling on the seafront with rather grand houses and small, mean dwellings between Durham Hill and Military Road. Some new streets had been laid out at the bottom of the Folkestone Road, but with little building. Biggin Street remained the north-eastern edge of the town due to the damp ground around the Dour.

Coming of the railway

The coming of the railway to Dover triggered another period of prosperity, making travel to the town from London on the way to the continent so much easier. Previously, travellers endured either a gruelling 12 hour stage coach journey or they could go by sea to Herne Bay and then by stage coach to Dover. The South Eastern railway from London via Folkestone opened in 1844, following spectacular engineering – the building of the Foord Viaduct across Folkestone and the tunnelling and cliff blasting between Dover and Folkestone. Horse drawn coach services to London were abandoned during the same year. A terminus station was built

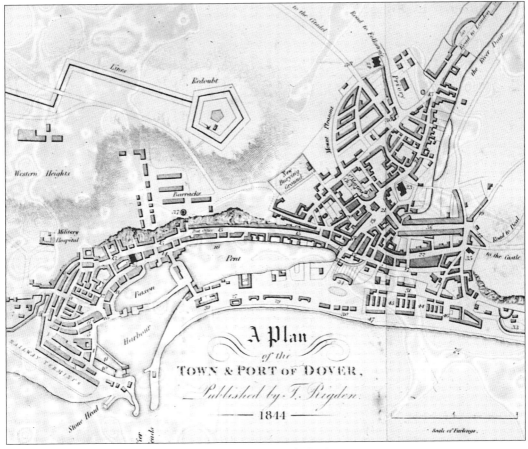

Small's Map of 1844

Building of the railway

Town Station

on the site of the Townsend Battery at Beach Street and in 1851 a grand hotel, the *Lord Warden*, was opened close by to accommodate cross Channel passengers. In 1848 18,439 people travelled through the port. This railway development removed houses in Beach Street and South Pier as well as part of Seven Star Street and Archcliffe Square. The arrival of the London, Chatham and Dover railway in 1861 had a greater physical impact upon the town with five acres required for the station and sidings at the Priory Station, followed by the extension into the Pier District and the demolition of many houses and public houses for the line and the Harbour Station. Later, the connecting line between the SER and LCD lines meant the loss of more homes in the Pier such as Round Tower and Council House streets. Yet more houses were lost when the railway was extended onto the Prince of Wales Pier in 1904 for the convenience of the Atlantic liner passengers.

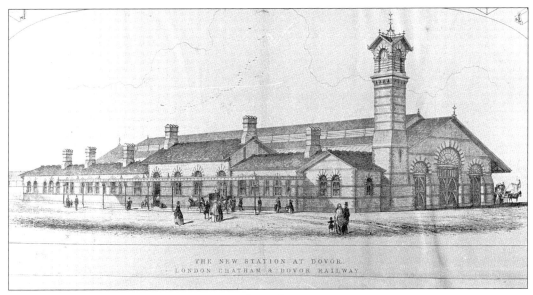

Harbour Station

Rawlinson Report

Edwin Chadwick, one of the great social reformers of the 19th century, produced a report in 1842 claiming that the labouring classes living in towns had a lower life expectancy than those living in the countryside. He believed that poor sanitary conditions, bad drainage, poor water supplies and overcrowded living con-ditions were the causes of cholera, typhoid and other diseases prevalent among labouring families. As a result, the new Liberal government in 1848 passed the Public Health Act that provided for the formation of a Central Board of Health with powers to create local boards to oversee street cleaning, refuse collection, water supply and sewerage systems. Soon, councils all over the country were enquiring into the state of their towns.

Dover commissioned Robert Rawlinson for such an enquiry. At this time the town's population was about 20,000. The Dover Pavement Commissioners had responsibility for applying the provisions of previous acts of parliament on the subject and their powers extended to Buckland, Charlton and Hougham. Rawlinson's description of conditions make horrifying reading today. There was no combined system of sewers and drains in many parts of the area. Better class houses had cesspools into which all the refuse of the house and the contents of water closets went. Other dwellings made do with an open tub under a privy seat, which was emptied at night into scavengers' carts. If the carts failed to appear then the tub contents would be emptied on the nearest waste land. In the Pier District the sewage was conveyed in pipes under the houses to a large tank, which emptied into the dock below the water line. Unfortunately, this system sometimes backfired, resulting in sewage flowing back up the pipes into the streets.

Similar situations prevailed elsewhere. In the parish of Charlton the 650 houses had no drainage. Main street paving in the town at this time was chiefly 'boulders' with pebble paving in the back streets. Rawlinson was critical of the Pier District and the squalid streets west of the Market Place were described as 'particularly evil'. The worst slums, however, were in Barwick's Alley and Paper Alley in Charlton and Manger's Rents (probably in Manger's Lane off Crabble Hill) described as a mass of flimsy shacks with no sanitation. The notorious Barwick's Alley had some 50 huts built one over the other on the steep hillside with only three privies and one well for drawing water, which provided a breeding ground for smallpox and fever. Even the better off told of sewage seeping up from under kitchen floors.

Water carts toured the town with both clean and waste water. Drinking water came from pumps and wells. During the enquiry well water samples were taken and were found to be contaminated by cesspool material and by the near by burial grounds. These were full to overflowing with the same plots being used again and again with many corpses less than three feet underground. The smell was overpowering. This led to the opening of the Copt Hill cemeteries, the first in 1855.

A clean water supply was seen as crucial and the report suggested that the three independent water companies should be taken over by the borough and a new waterworks built on Connaught Hill, drawing 2,000,000 gallons of water a day from 200 foot deep chalk aquifers. Construction began in 1850 and was completed in 1854. This was soon followed by a sewage works and main drainage system. Following the 1853 Public Health Act for Dover, £70,000 was spent upon a mains water supply with the whole of Dover connected over the next 25 years.

Other public services
The 19th century also saw other improvements to the town. A local gas company was established in 1821 under Castle Cliff, lighting the whole town by 1823. The gas works

Castle Cliff gas holder at East Cliff

Victoria Hospital

Trams in Snargate Street 1930

moved to Phoenix Lane in 1855 on what became the 20th century site of the recently demolished bus garage; by the 1870s gas lighting in homes was common. In 1881 electric lighting was introduced. Dover Hospital, later the Royal Victoria, was founded in 1850 funded by voluntary subscription. At the end of the century, in 1897, Dover was one of the first towns to introduce trams. Three miles of track were opened and the penny tram proved very popular between Buckland, Maxton and the Pier. In 1905 the line was extended to River.

Industry in 1850

The town at this time was mainly self sufficient and local industries abounded. In the harbour area were saw pits, a timber yard, ship repairers, coach, sail and candle workshops and a large oilseed mill covering three quarters of an acre between Limekiln Street and the cliffs. Two of

Harding's Brewery, Buckland

Buckland Flour Mill 1840

the numerous breweries were near the oil mill. In the Pier District almost every other building was a public house with 16 in a 700 yard stretch of Snargate Street, 30 in Limekiln and Strond streets and another 30 between Limekiln Street and Town Station by the *Lord Warden Hotel.* The area between Castle Street, Townwall Street and King Street produced consumables with two breweries, a cornmill, a malthouse, tannery and a velocipede factory. Above Castle Street was a pipe factory and Crundall's timber yard. Further up was a paper mill and in Charlton an iron foundry and flour mill. Still further up the river was Buckland flour mill and paper mill and yet another two breweries.

Oil seed mills

Harbour works

The construction of the Admiralty Pier between 1847 and 1871 finally solved the age old problem of shingle blocking the harbour mouth and was thought to be the first phase of the Admiralty building a great naval harbour enclosing Dover Bay. Whilst the ability to land cross Channel passengers on the new Admiralty Pier at all states of the tide helped considerably, the town was anxious to extend its commercial harbour beyond what had become Wellington Dock in 1846, Granville Dock

Construction of Admiralty Pier

Construction of the National Harbour

in 1874 and the Tidal Basin. Tired of waiting for the Admiralty to make a start on its great harbour, the Corporation obtained parliamentary approval in 1891 for a commercial harbour between Admiralty Pier and a new pier to be built to the east. A poll tax of one shilling per cross Channel passenger was approved to fund the construction. Ironically, before the new pier, the Prince of Wales Pier, was opened in 1902, the Admiralty finally decided to complete its great harbour. Work started in 1897 to enclose 685 acres of the bay and was completed ten years later. This extensive construction work between 1897 and 1907 had an impact upon population and accelerated the growth of the town:

	1871 census	1901 census
Builders	256	1753
Railway workers	186	590
Metalworkers	140	481
Merchant seamen	715	924
Clerks	39	311
Female servants	almost doubled to	2013

Rapid expansion of housing

Expansion along the western valleys had scarcely started by 1860. Building was beginning on the eastern side of the High Street. Large villas were built around Dover Priory, still a farm, in 1844, but Dover College opened in 1871 on this site of St. Martin's Priory. From 1860, beyond Priory Station, large, better class houses fronted Folkestone Road.

William Kingsford had purchased the former St. Bartholomew's Hospital lands in 1810 and the Shooter's Hill area was developed 1830-40. When the Wesleyan Chapel was built on Chapel Hill in 1839 there were no houses around it, but in 1846 the Latham Estate sold the area for building and Buckland Terrace was soon developed. The 1860 building rash in

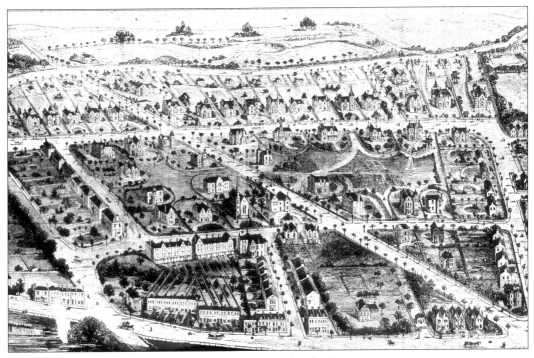

Plan of the Dover Castle Estate

Tower Hamlets crept up the valley as far as South Road, although the highest part was still a brickworks and was soon a working class residential area of terraced houses. The second phase, up to Goschen Road, began in 1896 with yet a third phase in the 1920s when council houses were built.

Dover Castle Estate

The Dover Castle Estate is part of the ancient Maison Dieu Fields, which had once belonged to the Maison Dieu, but after the Dissolution came under the control of the Crown in the shape of the Governor of Dover Castle. Lying below the castle and out of bowshot, they were used as a camp by the French besieging the castle in 1216. In the middle of the 19th century the Woods and Forest Department of the Crown decided to lease the land to the Dover Land Company for building. The estate is bounded by Maison Dieu Road, Frith Road, Connaught Road and Godwyne Road and intersected by

William Crundall in 1934

45

Park Avenue, Salisbury Road and Castle Avenue. In 1861 some roads were laid out but not built upon. Albert Road was first in 1870 and then the lower end of Park Avenue, but then nothing more until 1881 when William Crundall took out a 99 year lease for the whole estate. By 1898 the Castle Estate became an attractive residential quarter with tree-lined avenues and large houses with gardens to match.

Taswell Estate

The roads of the Taswell Estate were laid out in 1862 by Captain Taswell, but house building took much longer. This comprised Harold Passage, Harold Street, Harold Terrace, Taswell Street, Leyburne Road, Castlemount Road and Godwyne Road. This estate was also on part of the Maison Dieu Fields. Owned by C.B. Gorely in 1853 he wanted to start brickmaking, but following strong opposition the Town Council had vetoed it.

Folkestone Road area

In 1864 the Maxton Manor Estate on the east side of Folkestone Road was acquired by the Freehold Land Co. Two roads were built in each direction and plots laid out. By 1867 there were only 16 houses, 36 by 1887, but by 1907 the area was full with over 130 houses. The Winchelsea Estate on the northern side of Folkestone Road was built in 1866 and William Crundall built the Clarendon Estate between 1870 and 1878 on the Western Heights side of the Folkestone Road.

Barton Estate

Barton Manor, belonging to Dover Priory, once stood between the river and what is now Barton Road and its lands stretched across the valley to its farm in Coombe Valley. A farm existed here at least until 1840. Crundall laid out the Barton Estate between 1890 and 1900

Entrance to Bridge Street

on part of these lands, extending from Barton Road up towards the railway line to Deal and comprising Stanhope Road, Minerva Avenue, Mayfield Avenue, Nightingale Road, Astley Avenue, one side of Buckland Ave and Barton Road. The Barton Farm site itself is now covered by Beaconsfield Avenue, Charlton Avenue, The Grove and Limes Road.

Yet more housing

By the 1880s the Dover Gasworks had relocated to Union Road (1864) and working class housing soon spread around it. In Charlton there were rows of tiny

Victoria Park

working class houses between Bridge Street and Ladywell. In the old parishes of St. Mary and St. James there was infilling and redevelopment. By 1881 the fine crescent of houses named Victoria Park had been built as had Pencester Road and Maison Dieu Road with their large properties. In the 1890s the old Dover cricket field was bought by Mr. Adcock for housing and Leighton Road, Millais Road and the north side of Beaconsfield Road were built. 1880 to 1900 was a boom time for the town when the built up area doubled.

Number of houses 1801-1901

	1801	1811	1821	1831	1841	1851	1861	1871	1881	1891	1901
Buckland	71	119	131	157	250	315	377	463	588	839	
Charlton	48	114	116	315	501	606	761	1070	1298	1574	
Hougham	47	214	115	180	228	340	389	516	711	1052	
River	60	76	96	103	101	96	102	119	121	149	
St. James	255	272	272	372	521	630	685	709	759	716	
St. Mary's	1453	1508	1574	1723	1863	1895	1826	1737	1699	1695	
Total	1934	2303	2344	2850	3464	3882	4140	4614	5176	6025	7734

During the 1830s the town absorbed Charlton, Buckland and the urban parts of Hougham and Guston. In 1895 the borough comprised the parishes of St.Mary, St. James, Charlton, Buckland, parts of Hougham and Guston and, from 1904, River. Land north of Crabble Hill (where Buckland Estate is now) was included in 1921 and in 1934 the Eastern Docks and to the west as far as Lydden Spout.

Granville Gardens

Parks

The Granville Gardens were laid out by the Harbour Board in 1878 and soon became popular with both townsfolk and holiday visitors. Connaught Hall and the park of the same name were opened in 1883 by the Duke and Duchess of Connaught.

In 1896 a syndicate comprising purchased the land between Bunker's Hill and Crabble Road called

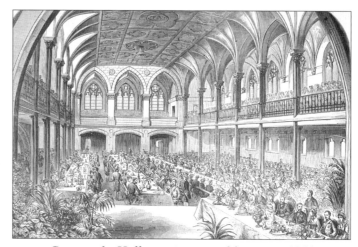
Connaught Hall opening grand banquet, 1883

Crabble Meadows to provide an athletic ground for the town taking in the existing soccer ground. It was opened by the local MP, George Wyndham, in 1897, but it was not a commercial success. With the threat of losing the facility to housing development the Corporation purchased the ground in 1902. Since then it has been home to Dover's rugby, soccer and cricket clubs with county cricket played there for many years.

Chapter 5

A picture of Dover at the end of the 19th century

An examination of Dover Directories for 1899 provides an interesting snapshot of Dover at the end of the century. It was, as ever, a busy seaport and cross channel ferry port with a population of more than 42,672 (in 1901) including over 2,000 military.

Town centre

Biggin Street before 1894 widening

Market Square 1905

The town centre had moved back from the harbour area of the Pier with Market Square, King Street and New Bridge now the banking centre. Castle Street was the professional centre with five of the 12 lawyers, two of the five dentists and half the doctors. Some shops had appeared in the High Street, which was still mainly residential with most food shops in Biggin Street and non food shops in Cannon Street. Snargate Street was also a shopping area. There was a

King Street 1906

Castle Street c1910

great variety of other shops including corset makers, watch makers, shoe makers, goldsmiths, bakers, fishmongers and greengrocers.

The Maison Dieu with the newly-built Connaught Hall adjoining was the civic centre. Several of its streets had been widened in the 1890s, including Cannon Street, Biggin Street and Worthington's Lane (changing its name to Worthington Street).

Snargate Street c1910

Cannon Street

Officialdom

It was a parliamentary constituency returning one Member of Parliament, having been reduced from two seats in 1885, and was a municipal borough, following the 1835 Municipal Reform Act, with a mayor, six aldermen, 18 councillors and three electoral wards named Castle, Town and Pier. The council met in the magnificent Maison Dieu, which had been converted into the town hall in 1860. The borough comprised the parishes of St. Mary's, St. James', nearly the whole of Charlton and Buckland, parts of Hougham and Guston and the liberties of Dover Castle. The borough's officers included the Town Clerk and Clerk to the Urban Sanitary Authority, Treasurer, Hon. Librarian, Surveyor and Engineer, Nuisances and Sanitary Inspector, Inspector of Water Fittings, Market Inspector, Collector of Rates, Collector of Coal Dues, Collector of Market Tolls, Town Sargeant and Master of the Porters. The borough's own police force, dating from 1836, comprised the Superintendent, Inspector, nine sergeants and 47 constables. The force also acted as the fire brigade. The town played an important role in the legal system, being the centre of a county court district and a quarter sessions venue. The ancient Court of Admiralty of the Cinque Ports also met in the town.

Public buildings included the Custom House, dating from 1836 on Custom House Quay, which also housed the Alien Office (forerunner of the Immigration Service), the police station was at the Town Hall and the fire engine station manned by the police was in Queen Street, the County Court in Snargate Street, the Inland Revenue Office was in the Market Square and there was another tax office at New Bridge. The Stamp Office was in Snargate Street and the Pilot Tower at the land end of the Admiralty Pier housed the pilots.

Utilities

The town had its own private gas company, dating from 1822, but the council-owned electricity works was beginning to make an impact upon the town with electric lamps from East Cliff to the Esplanade and in the main streets. The council also supplied the town's water from the Connaught Road works.

Banks

Dover was not short of banking facilities with the National Provincial, London & County, Capital and Counties, Lloyds and the Savings Bank in Snargate Street.

Newspapers

The people of Dover were kept well informed of both local and national news by five local weekly newspapers priced one penny: the *Dover Express*, owned by J. Bavington Jones, the *Dover and County Chronicle* (*and Kent and Sussex Advertiser*), the *Dover Standard*, the *Dover Observer & Visitors' List* and the *Dover Telegraph & Continental Traveller*.

Transport

The cross channel packet boats carried the royal mail and there was a large post office establishment to handle it. Dover was the base for 74 pilots who guided ships into the Thames. The inner docks could handle ships of 1,000 tons burden and on the Admiralty Pier passengers were transferred from ferries to trains. In addition, the town boasted three conventional stations: Dover Priory and in the Pier District Harbour Station and Town

Station, both of which had branch lines on to Admiralty Pier. The principal hotels were the *Lord Warden*, the *Burlington*, the *Esplanade*, the *Grand*, the *King's Head* and the *Shakespeare*. The town's porters were still active with 34 of them licensed to ply for hire, loading or unloading any carriages, horses or luggage to or from vessels or railway trains.

Burlington Hotel and Clarence Lawn

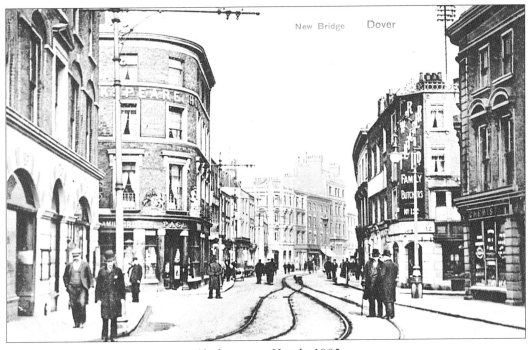

Shakespeare Hotel c1905

Esplanade Hotel

Holy Trinity Church

Getting around the town was much easier and quicker following the introduction of the corporation's tramway system in 1897 with three miles of track between Buckland, Maxton and the Pier. With four postal deliveries a day who needed the internet?

Churches

The town was well supplied with churches. The largest was the civic church of St. Mary's with room for 1700 with 1250 seats free, rivalled by New St. James' built in 1863, with 1400 seats, but there were also the Anglican churches of old St. James' (reduced to a chapel of ease), Holy Trinity, built in 1835 to serve the Pier District, St. John Mariners' Church in Blenheim Square, the new Charlton Church, St. Andrews at Buckland,

Old and new Charlton Churches

St. Bartholomew's Church

Christ Church in Folkestone Road built in 1843 and St. Bartholomew's in London Road built in 1879. The Roman Catholic Church of St. Paul had been built in 1868 and there were many other churches serving protestant denominations: the Unitarian Chapel in Adrian Street dated from 1820, Salem Baptist Chapel in Biggin Street from 1840 as well as another Baptist

Wesleyan Chapel, Snargate Street 1907

church on Commercial Quay. The Wesleyan and Primitive Methodists had chapels in Snargate Street (1835), Folkestone Road, Maxton, Peter Street, Buckland Terrace London Road (1839), Tower Hamlets and also met in various halls around the town. The Zion Congregational Church in Last Lane dated from 1705 and there was another in Russell Street. The Friends Meeting House of the Quakers was in Queen Street and the Jewish Synagogue was in Northampton Street where there was also a Sailors' Bethel. The Salvation Army was in Priory Road and the Gospel Hall was in York Street. In addition there were the two churches for the military: St. Mary in Castro and the Garrison Church on the Western

St. James's School

Heights. With most churchyards full, the dead were catered for at Cowgate Cemetery opened in 1835 and the Copt Hill cemeteries of Charlton opened 1854, St. James' opened 1860 and St. Mary's opened 1870. The Jewish cemetery was also on Copt Hill.

Education

Following Forster's 1870 Education Act, providing for elementary education for all children, the number of elementary schools had increased substantially: the National School in Queen Street, dating from 1798, catered for boys, girls and infants, Holy Trinity National School in Elizabeth Street (1834), the British School on Finnis' Hill, (1835), Christ Church National School, Military Hill (1842) for boys and girls with infants at Belgrave Road, St. Andrews Buckland (1842) girls and infants, St. James' National School in St. James' Street (1849) boys, girls and infants, St. John's, Blenheim Square (1857), Barton Road (1898) boys, girls and infants, St. Mary's Infants, Chapel Place (1870), St. Paul's Catholic School, Maison Dieu Road (1872), Charlton National School (1878) boys, girls and infants, St. Bartholomew's National School Widred Road (1880) boys, girls and infants. In addition there was the School of Art in its new Ladywell premises.

The Education Act had not destroyed private education. There were any number of private schools ranging from the prestigious Dover College boarding school, founded in 1871 on the site of Dover Priory to little more than front rooms in private houses.

Hospitals

Founded in 1851 and supported by voluntary subscription was the Victoria Hospital (not yet 'Royal') with 33 beds, coping with 260 in patients and 5,000 out patients a year. In addition there was an infectious diseases hospital at Tower Hamlets with 64 beds.

Less fortunate

The less fortunate in society were catered for by the Dover Almshouses built in York Street in 1824 which housed 35 and, from 1877, 20 in the Gorely Homes on Cowgate Hill. The National Sailors' Home, built in 1855 in Blenheim Square was home for 80 ship-wrecked sailors and there was a similar Soldiers' Home and Institute in Snargate Street. In Biggin Street there was an Anglican Home for Waifs and Strays and in Folkestone Road there was a training home for orphan girls with a Home for Little Boys in Templar Street. The Gordon Boys' Orphanage, founded in 1885 in St. James' Street, catered for 100

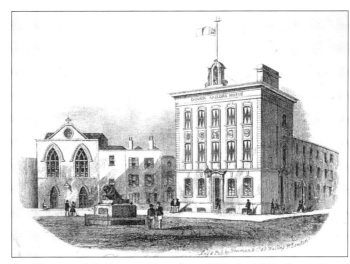

St. John Mariners' Church and National Sailors' Home

Gordon Boys' Orphanage

lads aged from 8 to 14. The Good Shepherd Refuge in Princes Street housed young 'fallen' women. To enable sick people to benefit from Dover's sea air there were convalescent homes at St. John's Road and Strond Street as well as the Seaside Orphans' Rest for London Orphans in Caroline Place and Liverpool Street. Two voluntary groups helped out the poor with food and fuel: the Dover Philanthropic Society distributed beef soup and bread whilst the Benevolent Society distributed fuel during the winter. As a last resort for the destitute, the sick and elderly there was the Dover Union Workhouse, which opened in 1836 in Union Road, now Coombe Valley Road, with room for 500 inmates and vagrants. Public baths were available in Biggin Street (now the Biggin Hall).

Leisure
In addition to its important cross Channel port function, Dover was an attractive seaside resort to which well to do London families came in summer with their servants to occupy sea front villas and hotels.

The sea front, which had been improved in 1894, boasted a fine beach with bathing machines to protect one's modesty as well as seawater baths. The bathing machines for ladies were opposite the Granville Gardens, whilst those for men were much further to the east. Swimming from the beach without using a machine was not allowed after 7am. The Granville Gardens with its band concerts, library and reading rooms were very popular with locals and visitors alike. The Promenade Pier, opened in 1893, was also popular. The scene was, however, changing. The Prince of Wales Pier was under construction by the Harbour Board and the long-awaited great National Harbour was being built by the Admiralty.

In addition to the sea front, Dovorians and visitors could promenade in Connaught Park, opened by the Duke and Duchess of Connaught in 1883. There were many clubs catering for sport including: cricket, lawn tennis, soccer, rowing swimming, sailing and cycling. Other clubs included the Dover Club, the Granville Club, the Carlton Club, home of the Conservatives, and the Working Men's Institute. There was a Youths' Institute with a gym, reading room and games room, which was open every evening for lads over 14 of good character, as well as the YMCA and the YWCA. Any number of hobby clubs also thrived.

The Tivoli Theatre, later the Royal Hippodrome, dating from 1790, was in Snargate Street, providing popular stage entertainment.

The more highbrow members of society were also catered for. The Dover Choral Union, the forerunner of the present Dover Choral Society, gave regular concerts. There was the

Promenade Pier

Bathing machines

Granville Gardens concert 1914

Dover Natural History and Antiquarian Society and the Dover Museum and Philosophical Institution, which was established in 1836 'for the promotion of Literary, Scientific and General Knowledge by means of a Museum, Library and Reading Room, Lectures, Conversazion and Classes'. It was the property of the corporation, but the Society of Arts nominated its curator. Meetings were held originally in the Apollonian Hall and the Guildhall Rooms until 1848 when the new building in the Market Square was provided with a covered market underneath.

Industries

By 1900 there were railway workshops, ship repair yards and iron works near the docks. Other industries included shipbuilding, sail and rope making, papermaking, ships' supplies, seed crushing and corn mills. In addition to many small businesses catering for every possible need, innumerable public houses and lodging houses, there were many larger and well known enterprises including:

Amos, photographer Snargate Street;
Beeching's shipbuilding yard
Brissenden, cycle manufacturer
Chitty, corn and oil seed mill, Charlton Mill;
Clout the ironmonger, Snargate Street;

Coulthard & Wilson, shoemakers with premises in Last Lane and Biggin Street with a
   factory in Chapel Place;
Court & Co., wine and spirit merchant Bench Street and Snargate Street;
William Crundall, timber merchant, Wood Street;
Richard Dickeson, wholesale grocer and provision merchant, Market Lane;

Flashmans

Chitty's Mill 1920

Steriker Finnis, timber merchant and brick maker, Biggin Street;

Flashman & Co., upholsterer, funeral director and estate agent, Market Square;

John Greenstreet, bootmaker, Bench Street;

George Hammond, merchants' and ships' agent, Clarence Place;

Hawksfield & Son, coal merchant, St. James' Street and Northampton Street;

Hills carriage works;

Igglesden, a baker in the Market Square and watchmaker in Snargate Street;

Kingsford Brothers, brewers, London Road;

Knocker, solicitor, Castle Hill House;

Leney & Co., brewers, Phoenix Brewery, Dolphin Lane;

John Lukey & Sons, wine merchant, Bench Street;

W. & E. Mannering, millers, Buckland and Crabble Mills;

Mowll & Mowll, solicitors, Castle Street;

William Rutley Mowll, coal, coke and lime merchant, Northampton Street;

Court & Co., Snargate Street

Edward Rutley Mowll & Co., wine and spirit merchants, Biggin Street;

Mummery Brothers, tanners and fell mongers, Castle Street;

Norris' carriage factory;

Oil Seed Crushing Co., Limekiln Street;

Prescott & Co., ship and insurance agents, Strond Street;

J. Scott & Son, steam dyers and cleaners;

Hubert Stiff, brickmaker, Maison Dieu Road;

Joseph Stiff, builder, Erith Street;

James Stilwell, solicitor, Register to the Harbour Board and clerk to the magistrates, St. James' Street;

Terson & Son, auctioneers etc. Castle Street;

A. L. Thomas & Sons, iron and brass founders, Dour Foundry;

Weston Lambert & Son, artists and photographers, King Street;

Worsfold & Hayward, auctioneers and estate agents, Market Square;

Garrison

Dover was the HQ of the SE Military District with a strong garrison based at the Castle, Fort Burgoyne, the South Front and Grand Shaft barracks on the Western Heights and the Tudor Archcliffe Fort manned by 'territorials' as we would now call them.

Chapter 6
1900 to date

Slum clearance and rehousing

By the beginning of the 20th century many of the squalid, back to back houses packed into the streets of the Pier District and the Durham Hill area were considered to be no longer fit to live in. Slum clearance began before the First World War. Following an inquiry in 1910 entitled 'Housing the Working Classes at the Pier,' the Local Government Board forced the council to demolish some Pier houses and to erect replacements. The 1911 Dover Corporation Bill gave the council powers to borrow money in order to purchase dwellings compulsorily in the Pier District and to improve the road system there. It was planned to widen Limekiln Street, Bulwark Street and Great Street, reconstruct Beach Street, provide a new street to connect Beach Street with Seven Star Street as well as a new sewage pumping station and outfall. The bill went through parliament but the Local Government Board included a condition that all the Pier people displaced over the previous 15 years should be rehoused. Consequently the council restricted its scheme to a modified viaduct and spur and the widening of Limekiln and Bulwark streets. Only 113 new houses would replace 311 to be demolished! Nothing was actually done until 1913 when contracts were awarded for the viaduct. Work did start on the Beach Street end of the proposed viaduct but with the outbreak of the First World War all work was suspended.

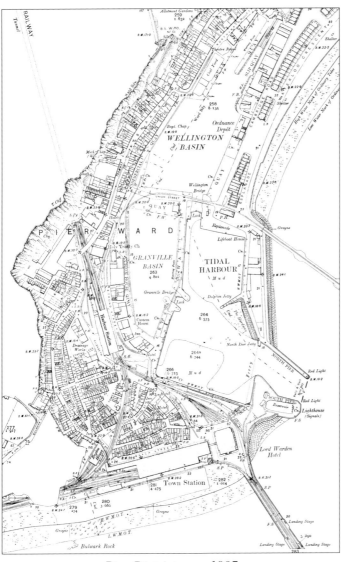

Pier District map 1907

Pier and Viaduct 1922

Mill Lane before clearance

At the end of the First World War the town's streets, tramways and water supply were in a poor condition and many of the town's old properties were considered slums, needing replacement. The council produced a slum clearance scheme and to build 1,008 new houses, including 600 on the slopes of Old Park, what we now call the Buckland Estate. At the same time the Ministry of Health that had succeeded the Local Government Board decided that no new houses should be erected in the Pier District, but instead should be built on high ground overlooking Shakespeare Beach at Aycliffe known as Ropewalk Meadow. In 1921 the Buckland housing scheme was reduced to 200 dwellings. They were not popular because the rates and rents were too expensive, particularly at a time when wages were falling. Extra private accommodation was being provided by some of the larger houses being converted into flats, including some in Waterloo Crescent.

Union Row clearance

By 1922 the Pier viaduct was opened to traffic at long last and the Limekiln Street bridge contract was awarded and work commenced, making the new viaduct temporarily unusable!

The Buckland Estate houses were completed in 1922 and those at the Ropewalk in 1923, which were then occupied by Pier people. This was followed by the demolition of one side of the Limekiln and Bulwark streets. Oxenden Street was cleared during the same year and the council decided to demolish Seven Star Street, Blenheim Square, Finnis's Hill and the north side of Limekiln Street.

With no empty houses and much overcrowding in 1924, the council devised ambitious building schemes, including 200 houses off Astor Avenue which were built in 1922 to connect Tower Hamlets with Elms Vale.

More council homes were built in 1925 in Tower Hamlets at Astor Avenue and Edred Road as well as at Shrubbery

Adrian Street 1935 before demolition

Cottages near Dodds Lane. More land was acquired for another 200 council houses. Whilst 30 council houses were built in 1927 at Noah's Ark farm at £541 per house, no further council housing schemes were recommended on account of cost, despite the demand. All the existing housing schemes were completed by 1928.

The 1930 Housing Act, however, required a 5 year slum clearance plan. This was submitted to the Ministry of Health in 1933 and involved the demolition of over 300 properties and the rehousing of 1,400 people in 355 new homes. Areas cleared during the 1930s were: Seven Star Street area, Finnis's Hill, St. John's Place and Chapel Court, Adrian Street, Mill Lane, Chapel Cottages, Pleasant Row, Queen's Court and the Hartley Street area. Market Court, Youden's Court and Mill Lane also went. The town council compulsorily purchased properties in Stembrook, Woolcomber and Trevanion Streets for demolition, which was interrupted by the war.

Properties in Durham Hill, scheduled for clearance in 1932, were not demolished until 1934; Blucher Row and Mount Pleasant were also cleared. The scheme in the Pier completed the removal of all the old property between the viaduct and Bulwark Street, which was started in 1913! The Limekiln Street flats were completed in 1935 and a start was made on 110 houses at the end of Union Road at the same time. A completely new layout was planned for the whole area at the foot of the Western Heights and the town council decided to build another 36 houses and two shops in Union Road.

With the dramatic events leading up to the outbreak of war in 1939 council house building at St. Radigunds was disrupted; houses started were completed, but no new buildings were begun once war was declared.

St. James' area 1935

Depression

The inter wars years were not a period of economic growth and the depression caused much unemployment, reaching its peak in 1932 with 2,624 out of work. Housing schemes absorbed some of the unemployed as well as the expansion of the Kent coalfield. One bright spot was the opening by the Borough of Pencester Gardens in 1923, providing a welcome green space beside the River Dour in the centre of town.

Second World War

The Admiralty took over the harbour for the duration of the Second World War, civilian cross Channel services were suspended, many businesses closed and thousands were evacuated. Consequently, the population dropped to 10,000. Dover became known as Hell Fire Corner and for good reason! By the end of the war half of Dover's housing had been damaged or destroyed by bombs or shells.

Bomb and shell damage
East Kent garage March 1942

Bomb and shell damage Wellesley Road 1940

Bomb and shell damage Randolph Road

Post war reconstruction

Sir Patrick Abercrombie's plan for a 'new Dover' was published in 1946. It called for the reconstruction of much of the building in the Dour valley over the next 20 years. The Borough Council sought to impose compulsory purchase orders on swathes of the town. Many buildings, such as the *Burlington Hotel*, were acquired by compulsory purchase and demolished. Much of the grand plan was, fortunately, abandoned.

Not surprisingly, at the end of the Second World War the most important problem facing the town was housing. Many homes had been destroyed whilst 800 others needed major repairs before they could be occupied again and by 1945 the much-reduced wartime population had risen to 30,000 as people returned. It was not possible to build any new homes during 1945, but 200 damaged houses were repaired and a site prepared for 400 prefabricated 'temporary' homes at Buckland Valley Farm, which Major Murray Lawes, owner of Old Park, sold to the Corporation in 1946. By 1947 these temporary homes were erected, but it was many years before these prefabs, as they became known, were replaced by permanent council houses on the Buckland Estate and at Aycliffe. The last prefab disappeared in the mid 1970s.

By 1948 new homes were being provided on the Buckland Estate to replace houses destroyed in the older parts of Dover. 'Poets Corner,' consisting of a number of new roads named after British poets, was built around The Lines there. Other new roads adjacent to the prewar council houses carried on the theme of being named after characters in Chaucer's *Canterbury Tales*, whilst most of the new roads and walks were named after Commonwealth or US cities, places or people.

Acres of land and some 150 homes were purchased by the town from the Crown Commissioners in the Leyburne Road and Harold Street area, where outdated houses were torn down to make space for council-owned blocks of flats.

Buckland prefabs pre demolition 1967

Union Road gasworks 1956

Dover Engineering Works, beside the Dour at Charlton, was allowed to expand in 1945 and again in 1955 by demolishing the Peter Street area. Badly damaged housing at Charlton Green was demolished in 1950 for a large factory, which was later occupied by the Royal Mail as an international sorting office. In 1952 contractors moved in to demolish scores of semi-derelict properties in Woolcomber Street, the St. James's Street area and at Stembrook. The gas works in Coombe Valley Road were rebuilt and enlarged and by the late 1950s an industrial estate had been constructed at the far end of Union Road, now Coombe Valley Road.

Demolition of war damaged buildings between St. James's Street and the sea began in 1948. The future of the damaged sea front area caused great controversy. Some of the properties were saved. Concern centred upon the war damaged houses between Wellesley Road and Douro Place. Many wanted them repaired and converted into flats but the majority on the borough council, later supported in 1951 by government, voted to demolish them and to build new flats on the site. In 1952, after much debate, Dover Council published plans for 300 municipally owned high rise flats there at an estimated cost of £500,000. One block was to be 15 storeys and 135 feet

Dover Engineering Works

Site of the Gateway flats

high, the other nine storeys. Dover Council decided that the design should be left to an international architectural competition in which more than 100 entries were received. Following comments by the Royal Fine Art Commission the Ministry of Housing demanded a reduction in the height of the two blocks to ten storeys and seven, resulting in a reduction in the number of flats from 300 to 223. After more delay in 1956 Dover Council accepted the tender to build 221 flats at an estimated cost of just under £1,000,000. The first piles were sunk in 1957 by contractor Rush and Tompkins and in 1958 the first occupants moved into The Gateway. As part of the redevelopment Townwall Street was realigned and Liverpool Street disappeared.

With greater confidence in the town the *Dover Stage* hotel in Camden Crescent opened in 1957 with its modern design, built on stilts with rooms and balconies angled to catch the

The Gateway flats and gardens

morning sun. In 1960 a national development company bought the land behind The Gateway from Dover Corporation. Planning consent was given for a 20-storey tower of flats on stilts with shops and car parking but, as so often happened, there was a government crack down on finance and a big increase in interest rates. As a result the whole scheme was shelved and the land was sold back to the town in

Buckland Paper Mill

1964. The site is still there, in use as a car park, awaiting redevelopment as part of the Dover Town Investment Zone.

In 1960 the Corporation vowed to provide another 1,000 council houses and flats in the following six years of which 300 would be on grazing land opposite Archers Court School on the boundary with Whitfield. By 1968 2,000 new council homes had been built since the war. The mid-1960s saw a development boom when a number of older Dover properties were demolished to make way for future construction.

Private house building was resumed with some 100 new homes on the hills at River and 39 off Elms Vale Road. A scheme was revealed in 1969 for the development of part of the Western Heights with homes, an hotel and leisure facilities. Fortunately for this historic site, the plans were rejected.

With so much war damage and demolition post war, population dwindled in the oldest parts of the town except for the blocks of new flats in The Gateway, Durham Hill and Stembrook areas. Many of the larger properties, especially in the Folkestone Road, were converted to bed and breakfast accommodation, catering for ferry passengers.

Industry

In the 1960s there were still a number of substantial industries in the town. Whilst Limekiln Street lost the businesses housed in the old Oil Mills building, following a disastrous fire in 1965, and Scott's, the dyers and cleaners, had closed after more than a century, the street still had ferry repair workshops, a mineral water factory and engineering establishments. The

Eastern Docks industries

72

Dover Engineering Works in the 1970s

Eastern Docks housed several industries on what was then a narrow strip of land at the foot of the cliffs: scrap metal, marine engineers, Parker Pens, Post Office cable depot and an oil installation, but with the expanding ferry business these were all removed by 1973. There were still a number of businesses along the river: Buckland Paper Mill, Dover Engineering Works and the London Fancy Box Company, which had moved from London in 1947. Another London business, Avo, employing 800, moved to a new factory at Archcliffe in the mid 1960s and a large telephone exchange was built behind Maison Dieu House in 1967. At the far end of Coombe Valley Road an industrial estate was developed in 1973.

Later in the century, however, local employment suffered two major blows: Dover Engineering Works closed in 1988 and the extensive site was soon occupied by a Co-op supermarket and a DIY store. Buckland Paper Mill, employing 200 workers, closed in 2000 and in 2006 plans were approved to redevelop the site for housing and light industry albeit with no progress to date.

Roads

The road layout of the town changed considerably between 1945 and the end of the century to meet the enormous increase in traffic travelling to and from the continent via Dover. Initially, this was concentrated on improving access to the Western Docks where most of the ferries berthed, but increasingly from 1953, when the Car Ferry Terminal opened, to the fast growing Eastern Docks.

All this traffic had to pass through the town. First Snargate Street was widened in the 1950s and premises on the seaward side demolished. This was followed by the widening of Crabble Hill and in 1967 London Road was widened from Crabble to Whitfield Hill. In the town centre a one way system was introduced in 1967 to help cope with the traffic. As a newcomer in 1974 I found it very difficult to find my way about town!

The Cause is Altered

1972 dig (now modern York Street)

Jubilee Way

With the increasing Eastern Docks traffic, the phased dualling of Townwall Street began in 1959, involving the demolition of the south side, which was to be complemented by a new dual carriageway, now known as York Street, to relieve part of the town centre of port traffic. This later project required the demolition of dozens of houses, shops, two schools, and several pubs, including the needless destruction of the ancient *Cause is Altered*, built on the site of Cow Gate at the top of old Queen Street. The new road was completed in 1972 after some delay to allow the excavation and preservation of important Roman remains by raising the road level.

It was, however, the opening in 1977 of the Dover bypass from the top of Lydden Hill into the Eastern Docks which finally relieved the town of most of the port traffic. This relief was, however, short-lived. Various controversial plans to link the Eastern Docks to the new M20 at Folkestone resulted in the vigorously contested decision to route the new connecting road over the cliffs from Folkestone, through Aycliffe and then along Snargate Street and Townwall Street. This major route, completed in 1993, virtually cut off the town from its sea front, creating constant noise and fumes, which Dovorians still have to endure.

Tourism

In 1970 work started on the construction of Dover Council's swimming pool at the Woolcomber Street-Townwall Street junction and by 1976 a £300,000 sports centre was opened alongside. Attracting tourists and their money became a priority and the White Cliffs Country image was adopted. Pursuing this policy the District Council took the controversial decision in 1988 to build a heritage centre on the derelict site around and over Roman and Norman remains off the Market Square at a cost of £14 million. The White Cliffs Experience,

75

as it was called, was opened in 1991 by Princess Anne and by the year's end had attracted 200,000 visitors. Many called it Dover's white elephant, but more than a million people had visited it before, with mounting losses, it was closed in 2000.

New Leisure Centre 1972

White Cliffs Experience 1992

1960s Burlington House dominating the town

Dover Town Investment Zone

Ideas for the comprehensive redevelopment of the St. James's area of the town, known as the Dover Town Investment Zone (DTIZ), parts of which have been derelict since the Second World War, were put before the public at an exhibition in July 2000. Thankfully, the plans included the demolition of the town's major eyesore – the derelict office tower block, Burlington House – plus the adjacent, empty multi-storey car park and hotel. The 12 storey office block had been built in the 1970s, but never fully occupied although five floors were used for some years by Customs and Excise. Many people were disappointed that the main feature of the final plans was a large supermarket and associated car park. A few retail outlets, a block of flats and an hotel would complete the development. Work on site finally began in 2008 with the demolition of the bus garage!

Expansion beyond the town boundaries

The villages surrounding Dover expanded considerably in the second half of the century with extensive private housing in Whitfield, River and St. Margaret's. This was accompanied by an increasing expansion of Dover activity into Whitfield and Guston. The first 'incursion' was in 1957 when Archer's Court, a new secondary modern school opened and commercial development followed in the 1970s when the newly-formed Dover District Council purchased land for light industry at Guston and also built their offices on what became known as the White Cliffs Business Park. New and existing businesses slowly occupied sites. The opening of Tesco's supermarket in 1988 with several extensions since means that most Dovorians now do their weekly shopping out of Dover town centre. The trend accelerated when Dover Harbour Board bought the 225 acres occupied by the disused Old Park Barracks for port-related activities, including recently a firm of Dover solicitors – although they do handle the Harbour Board's legal work! In 2009 the Business Park is set to expand again.

The loss of Dover's army garrison in 2006 after 1000 years and the closure of Connaught Barracks provides Dover with yet another opportunity to spill into Guston parish. A successful local campaign prevented use of the site as an open prison, but suggestions for leisure or educational use were dismissed in favour of 500 eco-efficient homes.

The townspeople converge on River and Temple Ewell to enjoy additional park facilities. In 1945 following wartime army occupation, the borough purchased Kearsney Abbey, built in 1821, with the intention of using the extensive grounds for much needed housing. The dilapidated mansion was demolished, but the beautiful grounds were saved for Dovorians and visitors to enjoy. Just across the Alkham Valley Road Dover Rural District Council purchased part of Kearsney Court grounds in 1959 and laid them out with an ornamental pond, naming them Russell Gardens. Dover District Council bought the adjacent property, Bushy Ruff, in 1974, providing even more open space and all enhanced by water features provided by the River Dour and its tributary.

Chapter 7
A Picture of Dover in 2009

Officialdom

Dover now has to share a member of parliament with Deal and the powerful borough council disappeared in 1974 when it was absorbed into the much larger Dover District Council. It gained parish council status, however, in 1996 and once again boasts a mayor and 18 councillors. In 2004 it purchased the historic Maison Dieu House, the former library, from Kent County Council to use as its meeting place and offices. In 1900 River was a separate civil parish, but in 1903 became part of Dover Borough, regaining parish council status in 1987, which it still enjoys. The independent borough police force no longer exists. Indeed,

the extensive police station in Ladywell built just before the Second World War is now little more than an enquiry point with local policing directed from Folkestone. The town has also lost its courts with the replacement of Quarter Sessions by Crown Courts at Canterbury and Maidstone and the loss of its own magistrates' court, except to hear cases brought by Customs.

Maison Dieu House in 1892

Utilities

The local electricity works, gas works and water company have all disappeared, replaced by privatised undertakings.

Banks

There are many more banks than in 1900 since many building societies have changed their status from mutual societies to banks.

Newspapers

Dover still boasts two weekly newspapers, the *Express* and the *Mercury*, although both are part of regional companies and neither are printed nor have offices in the town.

Transport

Dover's economy, as always, still depends largely upon its cross Channel ferry traffic. The phenomenal growth in roll-on roll-off freight traffic from the 1970s has made it more important than passengers and cars and has ensured the continued growth of the port, despite the competition from the Channel Tunnel, opened in 1994. The Harbour Board is now planning to meet an expected doubling of freight traffic over the next 30 years. This business is supplemented by the successful cruise liner terminals opened at the Admiralty Pier in the 1990s and by the temperature-controlled storage sheds for imported fruit at the Eastern Docks. Dover pays a price for this success story with the town centre intersected by the A20 dual carriageway to the Eastern Docks, causing heavy congestion and the accompanying air pollution. Ferry passengers no longer have the convenience of a railway station close to the port. Only a refurbished Dover Priory survives, awaiting the high speed rail link to London.

Churches
With the national decline in church attendance during the century a number of churches have closed, although there are still five Anglican churches in the town: St. Mary's, St. Martin's at Elms Vale, Charlton's St. Peter and St. Paul, St. Andrew's at Buckland and St. Nicholas on the Buckland Estate. The Methodists and United Reformed Church have one united church. There is a Baptist church and the Quakers still meet as do the Unitarians, but there is no synagogue or Salvation Army citadel. A rapidly growing, relative newcomer is The Ark evangelical church in Tower Hamlets.

Education
The school scene has been transformed during the century with the steady increase in the school leaving age. In 1900 schools provided by the local authority – elementary schools – allowed children to stay until they were thirteen. Dover at that time had no grammar schools, which in any event, were fee paying. Now children have to stay at school until they are 16, although most remain at school or college until 18 years old with about 40% going on to higher education. Most of Dover's elementary schools of 1900 have disappeared, whilst those that survive are primary schools catering for children up to 11. The 1944 Education Act established this change with new secondary modern schools catering for the over 11s. Dover's two grammar schools, dating back to 1904, survived the introduction nationally of the comprehensive system. A branch of South Kent College provides vocational courses. The private boarding/day school of Dover College still exists and, since 1906, the Duke of York's Royal Military School, albeit in Guston, has provided residential education for children of those serving in the army.

Hospitals
In 1900 the Victoria Hospital, funded by voluntary subscriptions, provided patient care for the townsfolk and there was the Infectious Diseases Isolation Hospital at Tower Hamlets. With the gradual transformation of the Dover Workhouse into Buckland Hospital soon after the Second World War, Dover had a local, comprehensive hospital service. Subsequently, the Victoria Hospital, which had become 'Royal' following the death of Queen Victoria, and the Isolation Hospital, which became the Eye Hospital, closed. Today, with the current trend toward fewer but larger hospitals, well equipped with the latest expensive technology, Buckland is suffering a lingering death and Dovorians have to travel to Ashford, Canterbury or Margate for treatment or to visit friends and relatives. A vociferous local campaign either to restore Buckland Hospital's former facilities or to build a new hospital partially succeeded with a decision to provide a new community hospital but without any overnight beds.

Buckland Hospital in 1960

Less fortunate

Whilst Dover today contains some of the most deprived areas in the country, the situation for the desperately poor has changed out of all recognition with the introduction of old age pensions early in the century and the Welfare State, including the National Health Service in the 1940s. The need for most of the voluntary and private institutions of 1900, as well as the workhouse, has gone. Despite this, there are still vulnerable, homeless and needy people who visit the 'soup kitchen' operated every evening of the year in a town centre car park by a rota of 200 people mainly from local churches.

Leisure

The sea front is still popular with people promenading, some sunbathing and a few stalwarts enjoying a swim in the harbour, but the crowded summer beaches of 1900 have gone. Most people now prefer a heated, indoor pool or foreign beaches with a barbecue in the garden on fine summer days. Pencester Gardens were not there to be enjoyed in 1900, neither were Kearsney Abbey, Russell Gardens or Bushy Ruff open to the public.

Since 1900, the heyday of the cinema has come and gone. The advent of television and later computers, videos and DVDs means that Dover has only one small, 100-seat cinema struggling to survive, instead of several large cinemas earlier in the century. There is no purpose-built theatre except for that within Astor College for the Performing Arts and St. Edmund's Roman Catholic School. The Connaught Hall in the Maison Dieu has to double as a theatre when it is transformed by the Operatic and Dramatic Society for its productions.

Roman Painted House

Amateur theatre is thriving with several local groups, including enthusiastic and talented young people's groups. The Dover Choral Society and the Dover Music Society add variety to the entertainment scene.

With increased leisure time for all there are innumerable sports, social and hobby clubs catering for every conceivable interest.

Dover Castle is now a major tourist attraction operated by English Heritage, although, unfortunately, local people have lost free entry to the grounds. Western Heights in any other locality would probably be as popular as Dover Castle, but it remains 'mothballed' by English Heritage except when part of it is occasionally opened by volunteers. In 1900 the Pharos at the castle was the only visible Roman remains to visit, but today the Painted House, which is just one small part of Roman Dover excavated since 1970 by the Kent Archaeological Rescue Unit led by Brian Philp, is preserved and open to the public.

The Discovery Centre, converted from the ill-fated White Cliffs Experience and built, unfortunately, on top of the town's important Roman ruins, provides a modern public library and adult learning centre with Dover Museum adjacent, housing the fabulous Bronze Age Boat, which was discovered under Townwall Street in 1992 by workmen preparing for the A20 dual carriageway.

During the course of a year, it is amazing how many other events occur from beer festivals and rock concerts to regattas and carnivals. This is clearly demonstrated at the annual Dover Film Festival when the previous year is summarised on film.

Despite all this activity, Dovorians desperately need a local tenpin bowling facility and an ice rink rather than having to travel to Ashford and Gillingham.

Demolition of the Packet Yard 1991

Industry and shopping

Dover has lost most of its industry. The ironworks, flour, paper and oil seed mills, breweries and tannery have gone as have the Packet Yard and Scotts Dyers and Cleaners. Replacements are few with the London Fancy Box Company and Avo/Megger Instruments the most notable. We have no shoemakers and the number of bakers (baking their own bread) has dropped from 35 to a handful. The town, with its reputation for having a different pub for every day of the year (never true), has lost many of its hostelries as part of the national trend. The innumerable shops in Snargate Street and from Bench Street to Buckland Bridge have largely given way to supermarkets and superstores with the premises taken over by estate agents, charity shops and amusement arcades; too many, sadly, are empty. We do, however, boast one sex shop! A successful venture is the De Bradelei factory outlet by Wellington Dock selling a wide range of clothes and items for the home.

Empty shops Woolworths

Garrison

Following the closure of Connaught Barracks in 2006, there is only one serving soldier stationed in Dover: the commander of the Shorncliffe Garrison at Folkestone also acts as the Deputy Constable of Dover Castle and lives in the superb apartments of Constable's Tower!

Regeneration

The town is still dominated by the castle on the one side and the Western Heights fortifications on the other. The medieval picture of a town and harbour hemmed in by the Channel to seaward and chalk downs landward, overlooked by the castle, concentrating upon its prime role of transporting people and goods across the Channel still holds good today.

Yet in 2009 Dover is at something of a crossroads with many empty shops in the town and heavy dependency upon the port for employment, but there is hope of regeneration in the next few years. Whilst the St. James's area redevelopment plans are a disappointment to many and unlikely to attract more people to the town, it will hopefully be an improvement on the current eyesores.

The Dover Pride Regeneration Partnership formed in 2004 recognises the relative disadvantage of Dover compared with the rest of the region, but has a vision 'that by 2035 Dover will be one of the most prosperous towns of the South Coast, characterised by a highly skilled and enterprising community that is proud of its town, its port and its heritage'. To achieve this it has a number of worthy aims: to improve access to the Port of Dover, economic regeneration, improving the education and skills of its population, tackling uneven social welfare provision, improving the housing stock and making better use of the town's natural and historic assets. This partnership includes Dover District Council, Kent County Council, South East England Development Agency, English Partnerships, Learning and Skills Council, Dover Harbour Board, English Heritage, Dover Town Council and representatives of local businesses and communities.

It is hoped that nine projects will help to transform the town. DTIZ has already been mentioned. The Dover Harbour Board's 30 year masterplan to meet the expected increase in cross Channel traffic envisages the redevelopment of the Western Docks area. In addition to four new ferry berths on the Prince of Wales Pier there will be a new marina alongside the Pier as well as commercial and residential development around the Wellington Dock marina with a bridge link over the A20 linking it to the town centre. Much of the historic harbour will become, unfortunately, hardstanding for cross Channel traffic.

Constable's Tower

The derelict Buckland Paper Mill site has planning permission for a high quality mixed use development with housing, community facilities, retail and office space. Hopefully, this will open up this stretch of the River Dour for public enjoyment. The extension of the present White Cliffs Business Park at Whitfield offers the main location for future employment. A redeveloped South Kent College campus may provide the

Dover Harbour Board's Masterplan

opportunity for a mid town mixed use riverside location as well as a boost for vocational and other skills training. Having succeeded in obtaining an extension of the high speed rail link from Folkestone to Dover in 2009, Dover Priory station has been modernised in readiness. The recently completed Dover Sea Sports Centre will accommodate a range of existing and new sea sports as well as hosting national events. The closure and sale of Connaught Barracks offers another opportunity on the edge of town for a quality development coupled with the restoration of the Victorian Fort Burgoyne and, hopefully, public access. In addition to all these major projects it is hoped to improve the general quality of the town environment as opportunity offers in such locations as the Western Heights, along the River Dour, Townwall Street, the seafront, Pencester Gardens, Market Square and Station Approach.

With so much dependent upon substantial public and private investment in the next few years we can but hope that all these grand plans will survive the present global financial crisis.

Seasports Centre

Appendix : Population growth

Year	Population
1801	8,657
1811	10,247
1841	19,369
1851	23,222
1861	26,333
1871	29,518
1881	30,270
1891	36,813
1901	42,672
1911	43,645
1921	39,999
1931	41,097
1941	No census
1951	35,215
1961	35,248
1971	32,850

River is included from 1903. From 1974 Dover borough became part of Dover District Council area. In 1987 River regained Parish Council status. Today the estimated population for the Dover Town Council area is 30,000.

PART 2

An A-Z of Dover's Streets, Ancient & Modern

Dover's streets have spread over the centuries without following any planned layout, but influenced by the restrictive nature of the site. From the original settlements on both sides of the Dour estuary and later around the old harbour, known as the Pier District, expansion beyond the town walls first began along the Dour valley inland toward Charlton and Buckland and eventually absorbed these villages. In the 19th century development extended up the dry valleys of Folkestone Road, Tower Hamlets and Coombe Valley before moving onto the surrounding hills in the 20th century.

Some of Dover's streets are still with us today after centuries of use; others have fallen victim to the coming of the railway, harbour expansion, slum clearance, war damage and the need for new roads to meet the demands of transport.

The streets and lanes originally became known from common usage, named either after a landmark close by or in the street, the main activity in the street, somebody's house or business, a tavern or where they led. Naming streets after royalty also became fashionable. The Tower Hamlets developers showed little imagination with North, South, East and West streets, but improved somewhat when making use of Saxon kings' names. The Harbour Board was fond of naming its streets after its chairmen. William Crundall, in the 19th century, named most of his streets after prominent Conservative politicians. The pre-Second World War houses on the Buckland Estate made use of characters from Chaucer's *Canterbury Tales*, whilst after the war names of some poets were used plus a multitude of cities and locations in the United States and the Commonwealth, emphasising their role in the war..

From at least the days of the Dover Paving Commissioners (1778-1848) street names have had to be approved by the local authority. In particular, efforts are made to avoid confusing postmen and the emergency services by having similar names in the same locality, although we are still left with Priory Street, Priory Road and Priory Hill!

In the following list of streets some have defied either name explanation, date of origin or location. Perhaps the reader will be able to throw some light on them!

Abbey Road is a continuation of Barwick Road and takes its name from St. Radigund's Abbey to which it leads beyond the town boundary.

Abbot's Walk was on the Buckland Estate where most of the streets built before the Second World War took their names from characters in Chaucer's *Canterbury Tales*.

Abbots (The) is a modern extension (around 2000) of Priory Hill. Sitting above the site of the old priory and on Priory Hill, this was a good choice of name.

Adelaide Crescent was on the Buckland Estate. It was part of the post Second World War housing estate where most of the streets were named after towns or locations in the Commonwealth or the United States, emphasising the role that they played during the War. It disappeared as part of redevelopment later in the 20th century.

Adelaide Place ran from Water Lane to Hawkesbury Street in the Pier District and was named after William IV's (1830-37) wife and dates from that time.

Adrian Court was off Adrian Street and its houses were built at the same time. It is listed in the 1841 census.

Adrian Row ran from the top of old Adrian Street to Albany Place. See Adrian Street.

Adrian Street now joins Chapel Place with Albany Place. Originally called Upwall or Above Wall, the latter appeared in St.Mary's Vestry records as far back as 1639. It was probably thus named as the street was above the medieval walls of the town, but was renamed Adrian Street to mark the site of Adrian Gate, one of the town's gates. Its houses were demolished in 1937 and replaced with new houses and flats.

Albany Place now connects Princes Street with Adrian Street. It was named in 1882 after the Duke of Albany, a son of Queen Victoria, who visited his brother, the Duke of Connaught, when quartered in Dover.

Albert Road runs from Maison Dieu Road to Salisbury Road. Named in honour of Prince Albert, following his death in 1861, the road was built in 1870 with terraced houses as part of the intended Dover Castle Estate, which was replanned later by William Crundall who built fine residences on it.

Alberta Close is off Selkirk Road. It is part of the post Second World War Buckland Housing Estate where most of the streets were named after towns or locations in the Commonwealth or the United States, emphasising the role that the Commonwealth and the US played during the War.

Alberta Way was adopted in 1982, but no longer exists due to redevelopment. It is part of the post Second World War Buckland Housing Estate. See Alberta Close for name.

Albion Place was by Chapel Place. The *Albion* pub, later renamed the *Carpenter's Arms* was close by and was presumably a watering hole of the builder. It is listed in the 1841 census.

Alexandra Place is off London Road. Princess Alexandra of Denmark married the future Edward VII in 1863 and this road was built about ten years later. It was adopted by the borough in 1891.

Alfred Place was at the top of Castle Street and presumably named after the Saxon King Alfred. It is shown on an 1851 map, but now forms part of Castle Street.

Alfred Road is off Lorne Road. Named presumably after the Saxon King Alfred, it was partially developed in 1897 by Worsfold and Hayward (and adopted in 1898) on the old Brook Ditch Meadow and was extended in 1936.

Alma Place was part of Charlton Green where it joined Peter Street. This neat little row of cottages was built during the Crimean War and named after the Battle of Alma. It was demolished to allow for the expansion of Dover Engineering Works.

Anselm Road is off Noah's Ark Road in Tower Hamlets. Built in 1928 by the borough council, it was named after an early Archbishop of Canterbury who was canonised in 1494. Following war damage, some prefabs were erected there in 1948.

Anstee Road, off Shooter's Hill, is a post World War II housing development and was adopted in 1980. The origin of the name is unknown.

Approach Road runs from Folkestone Road to Manor Road. Originally part of Manor Road, it was later given this name after a pair of cottages in the approach to Manor Road. It was adopted in 1922.

Archcliffe Road is now a continuation of Limekiln Street and both form part of the modern A20 dual carriageway. It was previously called Bulwark Hill. The road was so named formally in 1878 because it led to Archcliffe Fort, built by Henry VIII on the site of an earlier fortification built by Richard II in 1379. The name also appears on Eldred's map of 1641.

Archcliffe Square, Pier District was close by Archcliffe. It is listed in the 1841 census with many houses, but by 1898 had been demolished.

Armourer's Walk is only a pathway from Shipman's Way to Pilgrim's Way on the Buckland Estate where most of the streets and pathways on the Buckland Estate built before the Second World War take their names from characters in Chaucer's *Canterbury Tales*.

Arthur's Place ran from St. James' Street to Clarence Street. Taking the Duke of Wellington's Christian name, it was part of the demolished St. James' Street area.

Ashen Tree Lane runs from Castle Street to Maison Dieu Road. Apparently a large ash tree stood in the grounds of the dairyman's house that still stands. The lane is shown on an 1851 map and a dairy already existed there in 1671.

Astley Avenue is off Barton Road and part of William Crundall's Barton Farm Estate laid out 1890-1900. It was adopted in 1906 and commemorates a prominent 19th century Dover citizen, Dr. Astley, who was mayor from 1858-9 and provided an isolation hospital at Tower Hamlets at his own expense.

Astor Avenue joins Tower Hamlets and Elms Vale Road. It was opened in 1923 by J.J. Astor MP for Dover and named after him.

Athol Terrace and **Athell Court** are above the entrance to Eastern Docks. This terrace certainly existed by 1847 when a dispute over jurisdiction was settled. The court decided that the terrace was in the parish of Guston for ecclesiastical purposes but in Dover for municipal authority! Apparently a Mrs. MacIntyre purchased number 3 when these houses, beyond East Cliff, were built and suggested the name after Blair Athol in Scotland.

Auckland Crescent is off Melbourne Avenue and is part of the post Second World War Buckland Housing Estate. See Alberta Close for name.

Auden Way, off Astor Avenue, was built in 2008-9 on the site of Astor Junior School built in the 1920s. W.H. Auden, playwright and poet, was a regular visitor to Dover in the 1930s and wrote a poem about the town.

Avenue Road runs from Frith Road to Beaconsfield Avenue. The developers had presumably run out of names when this strangely named road was built. Part of it was adopted in 1894 and the remainder in 1906.

Baker's Alley or **Passage** is thought to have been the alley from Tower Street up to North Street. Apparently it was originally called Slip Alley, but in the late 1800s a widow lived in the end house and opened her front room as a sweet shop, which became known as Granny Baker's.

Baker's Close, now called Priory Hill, was part of the nine acres given originally to the monks of Dover Priory to establish a bakery. See Priory Hill.

Bakers Lane is mentioned in the Paving Commissioners' minutes 1838 and may be what was also known as Baker's Alley.

Balfour Road is off Cherry Tree Avenue. It was laid out at the end of the 19th century and named after Arthur Balfour before he became Prime Minister, but was already a well-known politician. Part was adopted in 1903 and the remainder in 1939.

Bartholomew Close ran from London Road to Chapel Hill and was laid out in 1866 by Mr. S Tucker on land formerly part of the medieval St. Bartholomew's Hospital.

Bartholomew Street runs from Churchill Street to Beaconsfield Road. It was built in 1882 on Bartholomew Fields where Bartlemy Fair was held until 1830. This fair went back to the days of St. Bartholomew's Hospital for lepers (founded 1152).

Barton Path runs beside the river from Charlton Green to Cherry Tree Avenue, which was part of the ancient Manor of Barton.

Barton Road runs from Frith Road to Buckland Avenue. Previously a lane known as 'Back o' Barton,' it was named Barton Road in 1879 and widened in 1891 when houses were built along it. It was in the Manor of Barton/Barton Farm area.

Barton View Terrace is off Alexandra Place and was built at the same time. Presumably, it once had a view of Barton Farm lands.

Barwick Road runs from the top of Coombe Valley Road to St. Radigund's Road and was named after the builder, Alderman R. J. Barwick, who was mayor in 1921, 1923, 1926 and 1927 when this part of the council house estate was built.

Barwick's Alley. Described by Bavington Jones as a notorious rookery, this cramped and insanitary old alley off High Street (where the empty Salvation Army Citadel now stands) was built by Mr. Barwick in 1823 but was condemned in 1875 as being unfit for habitation and demolished in 1882. Strangely, when smallpox came to Dover in 1872 none of the 36 residents was affected – a grim joke of the time was that the epidemic looked in but was afraid to enter!

Barwick's Court was off High Street in the 1875 directory. This was probably Barwick's Alley – see above.

Bastion Road, Western Heights was laid out originally by the military during the 19th century as part of the Western Heights fortifications and barracks.

Beach Street, Pier District appears on Eldred's map of 1641. Running parallel to the Town Station, which was built on the site of the Townsend Battery in 1844, the street was built on shingle known as Plain Beach where previously there was a beach road with fishermen's huts, shipbuilders' and sailors' houses. On the sea side was a pilots' lookout. The street was demolished 1910-1914 and reconstructed, but demolished again in 1976 to provide a parking area for ferry traffic.

Beaconsfield Avenue continues Beaconsfield Road to Barton Road. It was built on the site of Barton Farm by William Crundall soon after 1900. Lord Beaconsfield was the title taken by Disraeli, the Victorian prime minister.

Beaconsfield Road runs from London Road to Beaconsfield Avenue. The south side was built in 1882 by a Conservative named Tucker and named after the Conservative Prime Minister, Disraeli, who became Lord Beaconsfield. The north side of the road was Dover's cricket field until 1897 when the road was widened and the field built upon.

Beaufoy Road and **Terrace** is off St. Radigund's Road. They were named after C.E. Beaufoy, mayor of Dover and chairman of the Housing Committee when this road was laid out. It was built by the borough council in 1933-34.

Beaumont Terrace in Folkestone Road. Lord Beaumont bought Westmount in Folkestone Road and all the adjoining land, intending to found a monastery, but the project fell through and the land was sold and built upon in the 19th century.

Becket's Walk. Roads in the Buckland Estate built before the Second World War take their names from characters in Chaucer's *Canterbury Tales*. This walk on the Buckland Estate, built immediately after the Second World War, was named after Thomas Becket, the murdered Archbishop of Canterbury, whose shrine Chaucer's characters were visiting.

Belgrave Road is off the south side of Folkestone Road. Part of Sir William Crundall's Clarendon Estate, it was built in 1875-78, named in 1882 and adopted in 1901.

Bench Street is a continuation of King Street to Townwall Street. One of Dover's medieval streets, it was probably named after The Bench area which existed in front of Boldware town gate (on the site of New Bridge). This in turn got its name from a bench in the gate tower where people gathered to chat or transact business. It was the general market area for the town until 1479 and then became known as the 'pennyless bench' where beggars congregated. The street was widened in 1835-6 when shops were pulled down on the east side and rebuilt in their own back gardens.

Biggin Court was a cul-de-sac off Biggin Street inland from the *Salutation Inn* and disappeared with redevelopment after the Second World War.

Biggin Street runs from St. Mary's Church to the Maison Dieu. The reason for this name has been hotly disputed. The earlier name was Bekyn Street and from at least 1286 there was a medieval town ward of Bekyn around St. Peter's Church in the Market Place (where Lloyds TSB Bank now stands). Bavington Jones asserted that the word has a Saxon root meaning to build; alternatively a medieval word for a cap. Perhaps it simply marked the beginning of the town or countryside! Biggin Gate stood here until 1762. The road was widened in 1894 and pedestrianised in 1981.

Black Horse Lane, now called Tower Hamlets Road, took its name from the *Black Horse Inn* (now the *Eagle*), which stood at the corner with London Road. A turnpike was sited at this junction as was the public gallows until 1823. The houses were built on brickfields owned by Farbrace and Winthrop.

Blenheim Drive is a modern cul-de-sac off Dunedin Drive. Named in 1988, it was not built upon until 1990. Bearing in mind it is surrounded by roads named after Commonwealth or U.S. locations, it appears to have been named after the RAF bomber aircraft since there is no Blenheim in the U.S. or Commonwealth.

Blenheim Square was off Council House Street. Part of the old Pier District, the square was renamed when a Russian mortar was brought from the Crimea in the ship HMS *Blenheim* and presented to the town. It was placed in the centre of the square, necessitating the removal of an old red pump, which had given it its previous name of Red Pump Square. It was demolished in the 1930s.

Blucher Row and Street The Row ran from Durham Hill to Bowling Green Hill and the Street from Military Hill to Bowling Green Hill. The Prussian General Blucher was in Dover in 1814, staying at the *Ship Hotel*, when peace was proclaimed, following Waterloo. The houses, built around 1830, were demolished during the 1930s as part of a slum clearance programme.

Boston Close is off Roosevelt Road and is part of the post Second World War Buckland Estate. See Alberta Close for name.

Boston Rise was on the Buckland Estate. Part of the original post Second World War housing estate, it disappeared when the area was redeveloped. See Alberta Close for name.

Bourman's Lane See Last Lane.

Bowling Green Hill ran from the old York Street to Mount Pleasant. There was a very good bowling green here maintained by the elite of Dover and military officers, but it was built upon soon after 1834 and demolished as part of the 1930s slum clearance.

Bowling Green Terrace, like Bowling Green Hill, was built upon soon after 1834 but is the only part of the Durham Hill Estate, built between 1830 and 1850, to survive redevelopment. It is now part of Durham Hill.

Branch Street is now only a service road off Bridge Street. Before this street was built in the 1830s from Peter Street to Bridge Street there was a footbridge over a branch of the Dour. The street was subject to compulsory purchase in 1955 when the Dover Engineering Works expanded, but was resurrected as a service road when the ironworks was replaced by a DIY store and supermarket in the 1980s.

Bridge Street runs from London Road to Charlton Green. The bridge over the Dour was built in 1829, replacing a ford and the stretch of the ancient lane was then named Bridge Street. There had been some houses there for about 200 years and land on the north side was sold for building in 1828. In the early 1900s the houses on the north side were rebuilt as Matthew's Place, Paul's Place and Harveian Place. The first two were named after saints and the third after the *Admiral Harvey* pub!

Brisbane Way ran from Melbourne Avenue to Adelaide Crescent and was part of the original post Second World War Buckland Housing Estate, but was closed in 1985 as part of the redevelopment. See Alberta Close for name.

Brook Place ran from Peter Street to Brook Street. Taking its name from the Brook as the Dour was often called, it was already there in 1897 and was demolished in 1939.

Brook Street was a cul-de-sac off Colebran Street. The Dour, sometimes called the Brook, ran close to the street and both were later swallowed up by the expanding Dover Engineering Works. It was built in the 1830s on the site of St. Mary's Poorhouse, which was erected in 1795 but was closed and demolished when the Dover Union workhouse opened in 1836.

Brookfield Avenue is off Buckland Avenue. This new street on his land was proposed by Major Lawes in 1899 and was built upon 1905-12. Brookfield Avenue becomes Old Park Hill at its junction with Brookfield Road.

Brookfield Place is off Buckland Avenue. Built in 1897 by William Crundall on the old Brook Ditch Meadow and named accordingly or possibly after Brookfield House, which was just below Buckland Bridge on the east side of the river. This house was built as a vicarage for Buckland Church, but was never used as such.

Brookfield Road is off Brookfield Avenue and was built by Mr. Tucker soon after 1900.

Brunswick Gardens. This is a modern cul-de-sac off Old Park Hill, dating from 1970 and, despite being built by private enterprise, continued the naming theme of the close by Buckland Estate.

Buckland Avenue is a continuation of Barton Road to Buckland Bridge. It was built in 1891 on land acquired from Major Murray Lawes to open Barton Road to the London Road at Buckland Bridge. Behind this road was once a greyhound race track. Buckland, according to Hasted, the Kent Historian, took its name from two Saxon words: boc, meaning book, and land, meaning that it was land held by written charter.

Buckland Terrace London Road. Built upon from 1846, it was adopted by the council in 1896. Its houses are numbered 279 to 286 London Road, which it overlooks.

Bulwark Hill was a continuation of Limekiln Street on the hill beside Archcliffe Fort. A bulwark was a defensive structure, hence the name. Further up the hill it became Archcliffe Road.

Bulwark Lane ran from Hawkesbury Street to Oxenden Street and was there in 1850.

Bulwark Street is now a dead end alongside The Viaduct in the Pier District. The original street existed by 1750 and Bavington Jones maintains that it was named after one of Clark's towers built in 1495 on his pier to protect the Paradise Haven. However, it could also have been named after Archcliffe Fort or one of several bulwarks in the area i.e. Black, Green or Barley Bulwarks. Most of its houses were occupied by Cinque Ports' Pilots who had their old watch tower on the later site of the *Lord Warden Hotel*, built in 1851. As part of a slum clearance programme the houses on the south side were demolished in 1923.

Bunker's Hill Avenue, built in 1997, takes its name from Bunker's Hill Road that it runs into.

Bunker's Hill is off the west side of London Road at Buckland Bridge. It is named on an 1851 map. An obvious source of the name is the battle of Bunker's Hill in 1775 during the American War of Independence, but why it was used in Dover a hundred years later is a mystery. Perhaps there is a simpler solution that somebody called Bunker lived or owned property in the area.

Bunker's Hill Road runs from Bunker's Hill to St. Radigund's Road. It existed as a road before the council built houses on it between the First and Second World Wars, but does not appear in a Dover directory until 1948.

Butchery (The) was at the bottom of St. John Street and is mentioned in the Paving Commissioners' Minutes 1788

Butchery Lane See Fishmongers Lane.

Byron Crescent is off The Linces, Buckland Estate. Several roads on the Buckland Estate completed after the Second World War were named after British poets.

Cambridge Road is off New Bridge. It was named after the Duke of Cambridge and built in 1834 from Cambridge Terrace to the Wellington Bridge (Union Street). It now ends at the Dover Harbour Board car park. In 1906 it contained shipbuilding yards, rail ferry workshops, Crundall's coal yard and, strangely, Lambert's photographic studio.

Cambridge Terrace, built in 1856, was named after the Duke of Cambridge, a frequent visitor to the town. This fine block of terraced houses ran from Northampton Street, but is now part of New Bridge and Cambridge Road.

Camden Crescent runs from New Bridge to Wellesley Road. The Marquis of Camden was Lord Lieutenant of Kent and a member of the Harbour Board when this street was named in 1840.

Cannon Street runs from Biggin Street to Market Square. Mary Horsley claimed that the name derives from the Canons of St. Martin Le Grand using the street to service St. Mary's. Canon Ward existed in 1520 covering the St. Peter's Church/Stembrook area. Another explanation is that it is named after the Cannon family. John Cannon lived in the street below the church. Opposite was his farmyard and bakery where the *Royal Oak* later stood. John also owned a garden called Queen's Garden, named after Elizabeth I. John, who was mayor in 1716, was the son of Captain Henry Cannon, Deputy Governor of Dover Castle during the Commonwealth. Bavington Jones states that Captain Henry owned property in the street in the 1650s. Yet another explanation suggested by him is that it was named after Richard Cannon, Deacon of the Baptist Church, who owned property in the street. The street was widened in 1858 and again in 1893. It was pedestrianised in 1981.

Canon's Walk is a post Second World War path, running from Knight's Way to Squire's Way on the Buckland Estate, and was named after a character from Chaucer's *Canterbury Tales*.

Carlsden Close is a cul-de-sac off Crabble Hill and was built by Carlsden Properties in 1974.

Carolina Walk was part of the post Second World War Buckland Housing Estate, but was demolished in 1965 as part of the redevelopment. See Alberta Close for name.

Caroline Place was off Church Street. When the estranged queen of George IV returned to England in 1820, staying at the York Hotel, there was much excitement in the town – with some people supporting her and some the king. Edward Thompson, the mayor, had to read the Riot Act. The builder of this blind alley must have been for her! The street, off Stembrook, disappeared in 1954 following war damage and post war clearance

Castle Avenue runs from Frith Road to Godwyne Road and was laid out by William Crundall 1881 to 1883 on land formerly part of the Dover Castle lands.

Castle Hill Road is now a continuation of Castle Street, built by the military in 1797 from the end of St. James' Street to provide a better access road to the castle and to the Deal road rather than the old steep zig zag, which still exists as a public walk laid out in 1886.

Castle Place ran from St. James' Street to Castle Street. It appears on an 1851 map.

Castle Street runs from Market Square to Castle Hill. Built between 1830 and 1835 from Castle Hill, it did not provide access to the Market Square until 1836-7 when the stables of the *Antwerp Hotel* were demolished. It provides a marvellous view of the castle from the Market Square.

Castlemount Road is a cul-de-sac off Godwyne Road. Castlemount was a mansion with extensive grounds erected by W.J. Adcock for Robert Chignell in 1876 to accommodate his school. The grounds were terraced into attractive lawns, which were opened to the public sometimes during the summer. This road, apparently called Clinton Road originally, was adopted in 1893 and redeveloped in 1990 with modern housing.

Cave's Court was off Worthington Street. William Cave, a watchmaker and jeweller, had a business in Biggin Street in the 1870s and built six cottages at the rear with access from Worthington Street.

Centre Road, Western Heights, was one of several roads built in the 1950s on the Western Heights to provide housing for Borstal Institution officers.

Chamberlain Road runs from Northbourne Avenue to Hamilton Road. It was laid out and named by William Crundall, but not built upon by the council until 1925, retaining the original name. Joseph Chamberlain was yet another leading Conservative, a Birmingham industrialist, who became a Liberal MP in 1876, but later left Gladstone's government being opposed to home rule for Ireland. He led the Liberal Unionists into an alliance with the Conservatives, becoming a Conservative minister in Salisbury's government and splitting the party over the free trade issue in 1903. This led to the Liberal landslide in 1906.

Channel View Road runs from the modern Elizabeth Street and over the A20. Built in 1983 on the slopes of the Western Heights, its name needs no explanation.

Chapel Court was off Snargate Street. Possibly named after the Wesleyan Chapel in Snargate Street, this old court was demolished in 1938 as part of a slum clearance programme.

Chapel Hill was off Buckland Terrace, London Road. It was named not after the Methodist chapel built in 1839 (now the King's Hall) but after the Chapel of St. Bartholomew in the medieval leper hospital that stood on the hill, long known as Chapel Mount, until the Dissolution. An 1851 map shows the road.

Chapel Lane See Grubbin's Lane.

Chapel Place is now a cul-de-sac off Adrian Street. It ran originally from Adrian Street to Queen Street until slum clearance in the 1930s and took its name from the Baptist (now Unitarian) Chapel built in 1820. Previously it was known as King's Highway Above Wall.

Chapel Square (or **Plain**) was in the Pier District and is mentioned in the Paving Commissioners' minutes 1783.

Chapel Street ran from Adrian Street to Snargate Street. It appears to date from the building of the Baptist Chapel (now Unitarian Church) in 1820 to which it led from Snargate Street, but it may have existed previously as Upwall. It was blocked off and diverted in 1961.

Charlton Avenue is a cul-de-sac off Barton Road and was built around 1910 on the site of Barton Farm in the parish of Charlton.

Charlton Green is a continuation of Maison Dieu Road from *The Louis Armstrong* public house to Beaconsfield Road and was adopted in 1906. In ancient times there was a manor of Charlton attached to the Barony of Chilham mentioned in Domesday Book. No doubt this ancient village had its green here. Castle Cottages were demolished in 1843.

Chaucer Crescent runs from Roosevelt Road to The Linces. It is another of the roads in 'poets' corner' on the Buckland Estate, built after the Second World War.

Cherry Tree Lane/Avenue runs from Barton Road to London Road. Probably named after the original Cherry Tree Inn, which was already standing in 1814 and at that time was possibly the only building between Black Horse Lane and *The Bull* at Buckland Bridge. Cherry Tree Gardens were sold for building in 1872 and the lane was widened in 1895 and renamed avenue.

Chesters Court was between 43 and 44 Snargate Street.

Chestnut Road is a modern development off Elms Vale Road. It was built in 1989 and probably took its name from the chestnut trees in the adjacent Dover College sports field.

Chevalier Road is a cul-de-sac off Elms Vale Road. The Monins family held land in the Elms Vale area for centuries. John Henry Monins lived at Ringwould House when several streets were laid out in this area around 1900 and Chevalier Road was named after two of his aunts. It was adopted in 1938.

Christchurch Court is a modern development of flats on the site of the demolished Christchurch in Folkestone Road.

Christchurch Steps. See Effingham Passage.

Christchurch Way is a cul-de-sac off Dunedin Drive. Built in 1990, it is part of the post Second World War Buckland Housing Estate. See Alberta Close for name.

Church Court was off Dieu Stone Lane. It appears on an 1851 map.

Church Place was beside St. Mary's Church running into Stembrook. See Church Street. This old Dover street, built about 1840 and listed in the 1841 census, did not survive the Second World War.

Church Road runs from Folkestone Road to Elms Vale Road. Named in 1901 when St. Martin's Church was built to service the new housing development, part of the Monins Estate.

Church Street runs from Castle Street to Stembrook. First called Church Lane, running originally from the Market Square to Caroline Place, it was laid out following the demolition of St. Peter's Church around 1600. The land was sold by the mayor in 1590 with the authority of Elizabeth I to provide funds to improve the struggling harbour, but it is said that the mayor left town without handing over the proceeds.

Churchill Road runs from Maxton Road to Shakespeare Road. It was adopted in 1898 and may have been named after the poet whose grave is in Cowgate Cemetery, or after Randolph Churchill, the Conservative politician and father of Winston who died in 1895. If William Crundall built it, the street was probably named after the Conservative!

Churchill Street runs from London Road to Granville Street. Originally intended to be Paul's Street, it was actually named after Lord Randolph Churchill, father of Winston, who was a prominent Conservative MP when it was built in 1882.

Citadel Crescent is off Citadel Road, Western Heights. These houses were built for prison officers in the 1950s and the road named after the moated Napoleonic fortification near by which is now an Immigration Removal Centre.

Citadel Road is off South Military Road, Western Heights. See Citadel Crescent. This road was built after 1971.

Claremont Place joined Castle Street to Castle Hill. Named in 1879, it is now part of Castle Street

Clarence Lawn ran from Marine Parade to Liverpool Street. The Duke of Clarence, later William IV, visited Dover more than once, including accompanying the Russian Czar and the King of Prussia to Britain when Louis XVIII returned to France in 1814. Built around 1840, it was demolished following Second World War damage. The Gateway flats now cover the site.

Clarence Place is off Lord Warden Square. Apparently it was formerly called Crane Street, (and was so called in 1822 by the Paving Commissioners) or King's Head Street before being named Clarence Place – see Clarence Lawn. Running originally from Beach Street to the former Council House Street, it was partly closed in 1968 and completely closed in 1977 except to provide access to the *Cinque Ports' Arms*.

Clarence Street was a continuation of the old Townwall Street to Woolcomber Street. Originally called Townwall Lane, its name was changed to avoid confusion with Townwall Street. See Clarence Lawn for name. The road was closed in 1954. Excavations in 1996 found origins dating back to the late 12th century and from 1550 onwards there were stone buildings on both sides. The south side was eventually cleared in the late 18th century to build a large mansion, Clarence House, which was itself demolished to build the enormous Burlington Hotel in 1864, comprising six storeys with 240 rooms. After a chequered history, the hotel was damaged during the Second World War and demolished in 1949.

Clarendon Gardens were at the top of Belgrave Road and consisted of four dwellings. See Clarendon Street.

Clarendon Place runs from Clarendon Road to Birchwood Rise. See Clarendon Street.

Clarendon Road runs from Folkestone Road to Birchwood Rise. See Clarendon Street.

Clarendon Street from Birchwood Rise to Belgrave Road. Sir William Crundall built the Clarendon Estate and named it and several of its roads after Lord Clarendon, Foreign Secretary, who died in 1870 when the building of the estate began. Following war damage, some prefabs were erected in 1948 and replaced later with houses.

Cleveland Approach was off Roosevelt Road, part of the post Second World War Buckland Housing Estate, but was demolished in 1965 for redevelopment. See Alberta Close for name.

Cleveland Close is off Roosevelt Road, part of the post Second World War Buckland Housing Estate. See Alberta Close for name.

Cliff Court appears on an 1851 map between 93 and 94 Snargate Street.

Clinton Road – see Castlemount Road.

Coate's Lane or Cupid's Alley is mentioned in the Paving Commissioners' minutes 1778.

Colebran Street (called Colbourne Street) on an 1851 map. There were ratepayers of this name in St. Mary's Parish as far back as 1717. Apparently Ruth Colebran was a clerk employed by Isaac Minet, the banker, who made money from privateering ventures. The street ran from Bridge Street to Brook Street and was built about 1840 on the site of St. Mary's Poorhouse, erected in 1795, but which closed when the Dover Union workhouse opened in 1836. The road was closed in 1988 to allow Dover Engineering Works to expand.

Collins Lane existed in 1831and ran from Post Office Lane to Water Lane.

Colorado Close is off Winant Way, Buckland Estate, part of the post Second World War Buckland Housing Estate. See Alberta Close for name.

Colton Crescent, off Rokesley Road, was built in the 1960s and, like its neighbouring roads, was named after a tower in Dover Castle, Colton Gate.

Commercial Quay was a continuation of Northampton Street to the beginning of Strond Street. The carriageway was built in 1834 on the west side of what became Wellington Dock called Pentside. Previously, it was only a pedestrian way although an inn existed in 1793. It was taken over and demolished by the Harbour Board in 1929 to provide wharves and a coal and timber yard.

Common Square (or **Plain**) was in or near Council House Street according to the Paving Commissioners' minutes when paved in 1783.

Connaught Road runs from Frith Road to Castle Hill, along the foot of the park with the same name, and was named when the Duke and Duchess of Connaught opened the park in 1883.

Coombe Close is a cul-de-sac off Coombe Valley Road. See Coombe Valley Road for name. It was redeveloped with sheltered accommodation during the 1990s.

Coombe Road is a modern cul-de-sac off Barwick Road leading to industrial premises only. See Coombe Valley Road for name.

Coombe Valley Road runs from London Road to Poulton Close. Coombe Farm, originally part of the Manor of Barton known as Dudmascombe or Dead Man's Coombe owned by Dover Priory, was at the country end of this road and became the town's rubbish tip and in more recent times, an industrial estate. The road was called originally Union Road since it led to the Dover Union Workhouse built in 1836, but the name was changed in 1965 to improve the image of Buckland Hospital, which the workhouse buildings had become. Dover's horse races were once held in Buckland Bottom through which the road now runs.

Copt Hill see Old Charlton Road

Council House Street ran from Clarence Place to Bulwark Street. The Council House or meeting house of the Harbour Board once stood in this Pier District street. One of the earliest streets in the Pier, it existed by 1641 and was shortened in the 19th century by the construction of the railway line. The remainder was finally demolished in 1968.

Cow Lane runs from Elms Vale Road to Church Road. It did not appear in Dover directories until after the Second World War. Formerly a track presumably used by cows on their way to pasture on the downs, it was the home of the Elms Vale Laundry until a disastrous fire. It was then demolished and replaced by modern houses, called Kingly Way, at the end of the 20th century

Cowgate Hill runs from York Street to the foot of the Western Heights. The Cow Gate was removed in 1776. It was sometimes known as the Common Gate, leading to the common where the townsfolk could graze their cattle. Part of the common became Cowgate Cemetery and the rest was built over. The road ran originally from the top of the old Queen Street, but now runs from modern York Street to the cemetery.

Crabble Avenue runs from Hillside Road to Crabble Road (in River). Adopted in 1897, it was built upon in the same year as the adjacent Crabble Athletic Ground was laid out and opened. Crabble is an area round the former Crabble Farm and the existing Crabble Corn Mill, but the source of the name is uncertain, possibly from 'crabba' (a water rat or crab apple) or even from crabs found on the Dour there.

Crabble Hill from Buckland Bridge to the beginning of London Road, River and Crabble Road.

It was laid out by the Turnpike Commissioners in the 18th century. The lower end was widened in 1955. See Crabble Avenue for name.

Crabble Meadows is a public road and then path from Buckland Bridge to Crabble Avenue over what were water meadows of the adjacent Dour. It provides access to St. Andrews Church.

Crafford Street runs from Dour Street to Maison Dieu Road. Mary Horsley claimed that it was planned by a builder named Crafford in 1868, but Bavington Jones and Terry Sutton maintain that it was named after John Crafford, Master of the Maison Dieu in Henry VIII's reign. The corporation agreed the name in 1861.

Crane Street appears on Eldred's map of 1641 and was possibly named after a primitive unloading crane. It is the earliest name for Clarence Place in the Pier District, which was also once called King's Head Street after a public house dating from James I. See Clarence Place.

Cross Place. This name is given in some ancient documents to the Market Square where a cross was erected during fairs to signify that fairs originally had a religious character.

Crosswall ran from Union Street to Custom House Quay. Built upon the crosswall, which was constructed in 1661 to divide what became the Granville Dock from the Tidal Basin, it was rebuilt in 1737. It lost its houses with the coming of the railway, retaining only a fish market. Taken over by the Harbour Board it was closed to the public in 1954. Union Street was also once called Crosswall – being a damming wall built in 1583 to enclose the Pent (later the Wellington Dock).

Crown Court ran from St. James Street to Townwall Street.

Cupid's Alley or Coate's Lane is mentioned in the Paving Commissioners' minutes 1778. I wonder how it got its nickname?

Curlings Lane is mentioned in the Paving Commissioners' Minutes 1786.

Curzon Road is a cul-de-sac off South Road, Tower Hamlets and was built by 1912. Lord Curzon of Kedleston, a former Viceroy of India, was appointed Lord Warden of the Cinque Ports in 1904, but soon resigned and was replaced by the Prince of Wales in 1905. He later held a number of senior government posts.

Custom House Quay faced the Granville Dock. The original quay probably dates from 1670, but the Custom House, which gave the quay its name, stood there from 1682 and was rebuilt in 1806. In 1922 Customs moved its HQ to the sea front. The formation of the quay began about 1670 when houses and warehouses were built on the eastern side of Strond Street and private quays were constructed in front of them. It ran from Strond Street to Crosswall, but was virtually derelict by 1939 and was taken over by the Harbour Board, closed to the public and cleared of buildings in 1949.

Danes Court is off Old Charlton Road. Castell Dane was a medieval ward of Dover but 'the Danes' were not in it! The name may come from 'Dens', a Saxon word for a clearing in the woods. The 20th century estate was built on the land.

De Burgh Hill is off Templar Street and De Burgh Street runs from Tower Hamlets Road to the

Hill. De Burgh Street was built in 1864 and De Burgh Hill in 1897. They were named after Hubert de Burgh, Constable of Dover Castle in the reigns of King John and Henry III. He was also Lord Warden of the Cinque Ports and founded the Maison Dieu in 1203 for the reception of pilgrims.

Delaware Dell was part of the post Second World War Buckland Housing Estate. This path was closed when houses eventually replaced post war prefabs. See Alberta Close for name.

Devonshire Road is a cul-de-sac off Goschen Road. Laid out in 1906, it was named by William Crundall after a prominent politician of the time, the Duke of Devonshire. Houses were not built upon it until 1927 when council houses were constructed.

Dickson Road is off Tower Hamlets Road. This street, the last to be built in Tower Hamlets, was built in 1890 by William Crundall and named after Major Alexander Dickson, MP for Dover 1865-1889 who married Lady North of the Waldershare family.

Dieu Stone Lane is off Maison Dieu Road. This old lane originally ran from St. Mary's Church to Maison Dieu Road and marked the boundary of the Maison Dieu lands. For many years it was apparently called Dee Stone Lane since there was a boundary stone with a D on it.

Dodd's Lane is off Crabble Hill. John Dodd, a brickmaker, built Dodd's House and 12 other houses in 1808. The lane was not formally named until 1879. His ownership of this land was the subject of an unusual court case in 1842. He showed his deeds to George Hudson, notorious for claiming ownership of property. Hudson took the deeds but never returned them and was later sentenced to seven years imprisonment. Unfortunately, Dodd died before the case was heard.

Dolphin Court was off Dolphin Lane. See Dolphin Lane.

Dolphin Lane is now only a short stretch off Russell Street meeting part of the modern St. James's Street around the multi-storey car park. It was once an important route from the town to the castle with the *Dolphin* public house, but the street name may well be a corruption of Dauphin, recalling the siege of the castle by the French Dauphin in 1216; alternatively, a dolphin was a mooring post for ships. A 1737 map shows it as Turnpike Lane. Until the Second World War it ran from the Market Square to Russell Street, but suffered war damage and lost its buildings and its access to Market Square.

Dolphin Passage ran from Castle Street to Dolphin Lane. See Dolphin Lane.

Dolphin Place was off Dolphin Lane. See Dolphin Lane

Douglas Road runs from Goschen Road to South Road in Tower Hamlets. It was laid out by George Lewis in 1895 but may have been built upon by William Crundall in 1906, when it was named after an East Kent Conservative MP.

Dour Street links Park Street to Crafford Street. Running parallel to the River Dour, this attractive terraced street was built on Wood's Meadow in 1859. A proposal to call it Gore Street after the Gorleys who lived at Ladywell Farm for many years did not succeed. Instead it was apparently named after John Crafford, Master of the Maison Dieu in Henry VIII's reign. It was adopted in 1868.

Douro Place is now a cul-de-sac off Marine Parade curtailed by the A20. This road originally ran from Marine Parade to Liverpool Street. Douro was a Spanish title given to the Duke of Wellington following his successes in Spain. Wellington, in addition to being Prime Minister was Lord Warden of the Cinque Ports from 1830 and Chairman of the Harbour Board until his death in 1851.

Drop Redoubt Road is off Bastion Road, Western Heights. It is close to the Drop Redoubt, part of the 19th century fortifications. The Redoubt takes its name from the large mass of stone and mortar on the site, known as the Bredenstone, which is the remains of a Roman lighthouse and known locally as the 'devil's drop of mortar'.

Dryden Road is off The Linces, Buckland Estate. Built in 1948, it was one of several roads on the Buckland Estate completed in the late 1940s and named after British poets.

Dunedin Drive is off Melbourne Avenue. Part of the post Second World War Buckland Housing Estate, it dates from 1988. See Alberta Close for name.

Durban Crescent is off Melbourne Avenue and part of the post Second World War Buckland Housing Estate. See Alberta Close for name.

Durham Close is off Durham Hill. It forms part of the post Second World War redevelopment of the Durham Hill area. See Durham Hill for the name.

Durham Hill runs from York Street to Military Road. It road ran originally from the old York Street to Mount Pleasant. Building began in the late 1820s and John George Lambton, Lord Privy Seal, was created a baron in 1828 and Earl of Durham in 1833. Most of the Durham Hill area was demolished in the 1930s as part of the Corporation's slum clearance programme.

Durham Place ran from Durham Hill to Mount Pleasant and was built at the same time. See Durham Hill.

East Cliff runs from Townwall Street to Athol Terrace. Before the 19th century there were no buildings at the eastern end of the sea front, only a bank of shingle over which John Smith trudged to reach his peculiar home, known as Smith's Folly, an upturned boat. Running behind Marine Parade, there are fine buildings dating from 1834 on its south side, fronting the sea, with modest terraced cottages dating from 1817 backing on to the towering east cliff.

East Street runs from Tower Hamlets Road to Widred Road. See Tower Hamlets Road. At least this street, built in 1865, was named correctly according to the compass, unlike West Street, North Street and South Road.

Eastbrook Place appears on maps between 1850 and 1900, but is now part of Maison Dieu Road from Dieu Stone Lane to Castle Street. The eastern branch of the Dour emptied into the sea near here. It was formerly called Maison Dieu Place.

Eaton Road runs from Elms Vale Road to Astor Avenue. The Eatons were merchants in the town and three of them were mayors in the 17th century. There are monuments to them in St. Mary's Church. The last of the male line, Peter Eaton, died in 1769. He was the grandson of Sir Peter Eaton, who died in 1730 aged 75, and great grandson of Captain Nicholas Eaton of Dover.

Terry Sutton's research, however, reveals that the road was named after a member of the Monins family who held land in the Elms Vale area for centuries. John Henry Monins lived at Ringwould House when several streets were laid out in this area around 1900 and Eaton Road was named after his son, John Eaton Monins. The road was adopted in 1903.

Eaves Road is off Markland Road in Elms Vale. Tom Eaves was a popular master at St. Martin's School killed during the First World War. He was also scoutmaster of the local troop and when, later, they built headquarters behind Markland Road it was named Eaves Hall. Some houses were then built and the road took the name. It was adopted in 1974.

Edgar Road runs from Coombe Valley Road to Prospect Place. Edgar, King of the English, reigned from 959 to 975.By one of his laws the Borough Court was held three times a week until the 19th century when Quarter Sessions replaced it. Prior to 1875 the road was called Edgar Place.

Edred Road runs from Noah's Ark Road to Widred Road. Built in 1865, it was named after the King of the English from 946 to 955. Following war damage, prefabs were erected in 1948. See Tower Hamlets Road.

Edwards Road is off Biggin Street. Named after Revd. E. Edwards, Salem Baptist Church minister 1878-1905, it was purchased in 1906 and became a public road.

Effingham Crescent runs from Priory Road to Dover College. Originally called St. Martin's Street, it was built by Parker Ayers in 1847. Lady Effingham was a frequent visitor to Dover and contributed to the cost of building Christchurch, which was built at about the same time as the Crescent.

Effingham Passage connects the Folkestone and Military roads for pedestrians. Probably dating from the construction of Military Road and ending opposite Effingham Street, these steps are now called Christchurch Steps since they were adjacent to Christchurch until it was demolished.

Effingham Place was on the corner of Folkestone Road and Effingham Street and built at the same time. See Effingham Street.

Effingham Street is off Folkestone Road beside Dover College. It was called St. Martin's Street from 1847-1872 and was renamed after Lady Effingham, a frequent visitor to Dover.

Elizabeth Street is off Limekiln Street. Apparently Thomas Digges built a sluice and store with an effigy of Elizabeth I upon it at the end of the street in 1590. It was once an important thoroughfare from Limekiln Street to Hawkesbury Street in the Pier District and contained meeting places for Wesleyans, Roman Catholics and Jews. One side was demolished to make way for Harbour Station in 1860; now it hardly exists except to provide access to a water pumping station and to Channel View Road.

Elm Park Gardens is a cul-de-sac off Reading Road. It was built in 1965 and takes its name from Elms Vale.

Elms Vale Road is a fork off Folkestone Road. The Elms valley and lane leading to Hougham was renowned for its elm trees. Originally called Elms Road it dates from 1898 and by 1906 it was only built upon up to the *Crown and Sceptre*.

Elsam's Cottages were off Dieu Stone Lane. Richard Elsam was the town architect who built the gaol in Gaol Lane and apparently built this row of cottages in 1820 from left over materials. His best known work has also disappeared, the Round House, built in Townwall Street for John Shipdem, Town Clerk.

Elves Lane is in Joe Harman's list of Dover Streets. There was a Paving Commissioner named Henry Elve who had a hand in developing Castle Street, which could explain the name.

Endeavour Place was off London Road, Buckland. Along with the public house the *Old Endeavour*, it takes its name from a privateer fitted out in Dover in 1746. This passage was not named until 1879.

Ennismore Gardens see Salisbury Road.

Eric Road runs from London Road to Oswald Road, Buckland. Built in 1871, it is named after the last Viking king of York, Eric Bloodaxe, who was killed by King Edred of Kent in 954.

Erith Street is off Buckland Terrace, London Road. Built by 1839, it was named by James Beale who came from Erith and built the house, Erith Place, at the end of the road.

Esplanade (The) is now the stretch of the sea front from Harbour House to the Prince of Wales Pier. Laid out in 1833 on the shingle ridge westwards from Waterloo Crescent, it included the Esplanade Hotel. It was curtailed in 1977 when the hoverport was constructed.

Ethelbert Road runs from South Road to East Street. It was built in 1865 and named after a king of Kent 560-616, the first English king to convert to Christianity, following the arrival of St. Augustine in 597. See Tower Hamlets Road.

Evison Close is off Parfitt Way. It was built in 1995 and named after Professor Vera Evison, an archaeologist who helped with the excavation of an Anglo-Saxon cemetery on the site in 1994 when 200 graves were found.

Exhibition Place was a row of houses in Woolcomber Street. These houses were built in 1851, the year of the Great Exhibition.

Farthingloe Road is off Manor Rise, Maxton. Matilda de Ffarninglo held Manor Court Farm from the Prior of Dover during Henry VIII's reign. Part of the road was adopted in 1952 and the remainder in 1956. The name means hill of the fern dwellers.

Fector's Place ran from Russell Street to St. James's Street. Built in 1835 on the boundary of the gardens belonging to the house of Mr. Peter Fector, the banker, in St. James's Street. It is now part of Russell Street.

Fifteen Post Lane – see Samson's Lane, ran from Snargate Street to Paradise Pent and is mentioned in Paving Commissioners' minutes 1783.

Finnis's Court was off Finnis's Hill. See Finnis's Hill.

Finnis's Hill was off Limekiln Street. On this hill stood the home, workshop and yard of Mr. Finnis, a builder, until about 1830. Before that it was called Upper Walton Lane. The lower lane led from Strond Street to Limekiln Street. Robert Finnis, his son John and his grandson Steriker were all mayors of Dover. The area was demolished in the 1930s as part of a slum clearance programme. The road was closed in 1971.

Finnis's Place was off Finnis's Hill.

Fishermen's Row appears on a 1737 map and was on the beach in the Pier District.

Fishmongers Lane runs from King Street to Mill Lane. Near the Townwall Street entrance to this old lane, once called King's Lane, stood Fishers Gate where fishermen washed their nets in the river. A small fish market was built in 1831 on one side, which was later replaced by an ice store. Bavington Jones states that it was previously called Butchery Lane where there was doubtless a slaughterhouse.

Five Post Lane connected Adrian Street with Snargate Street. This steep lane originally had five posts spread across it to allow only pedestrians through. It existed before 1841.

Florida Close is off Roosevelt Road and part of the post Second World War Buckland Housing Estate. See Alberta Close for name.

Florida Way was a path off Roosevelt Road and part of the post Second World War Buckland Housing Estate, but was demolished in 1965. See Alberta Close for name.

Flying Horse Lane now runs from King Street to St. James's Street. Once called St. James's Lane, the *Flying Horse Inn* was in this lane and was previously called the *Fleur de Lis*. Richard Dawkes is said to have owned the inn when he and eleven others seized the castle during the Commonwealth. It ran from King Street to St. James' Lane until post Second World War redevelopment.

Folkestone Road now runs into the Priory Road/York Street roundabout. It was opened as a road to Folkestone in 1762 under the Turnpike Acts, although a King's Highway existed on this road line from at least 1274 to Elms Vale and Hougham. The toll gate was at the junction with Elms Vale Road until demolished in 1877. St. Martin's Hill (the stretch between Priory Gate Road and Priory Road) was developed in 1843. Beyond mostly dates from about 1860 to the end of the century. The road was originally a continuation of Priory Street, but was curtailed by the construction of the York Street dual carriageway in the 1970s.

Fort Hill led up to Archcliffe Fort, now part of the A20.

Fountain Lane is mentioned in the Paving Commissioners' Minutes 1822. Was it by the *Fountain* pub now called the *Sportsman* in London Road?

Fox Passage was between Townwall Street and St. James's Street. Once a narrow right of way, it probably took its name from Thomas Fox, a well known local lawyer who lived at 2 Townwall Street. It is now part of Russell Street.

Franklin's Walk is off Parson's Way, part of the post Second World War Buckland Housing

Estate. See Alberta Close for name.

Freeman's Cottages. Previously called Reynold's Court, Mr. R. Freeman renamed this row of four cottages which once stood on the present site of Woolworths. Mr. Freeman had a tailor's shop in front of the cottages. This is thought to be the site of Priory Farm before the Dissolution. Built into the front of the cottages was a pair of scales and three sheaves of wheat made of tiles as a symbol of fair dealing.

Friar's Way runs from Pilgrim's Way to Weaver's Way. All the roads in the Buckland Estate built before the Second World War take their names from characters in Chaucer's *Canterbury Tales*.

Frith Road runs from Charlton Green to Connaught Road. It was originally called Love Lane until it was widened and built upon in 1883. At its junction with Barton Road it becomes Old Charlton Road leading eventually via a track to Frith Farm at the top of the hill.

Fulbert Road is off Melbourne Avenue. It was built by the council in the 1960s almost on the boundary of Dover and Whitfield. It was named after Fulbert Tower in Dover Castle, which in turn was named after Fulbert of Dover, Lord of Chilham, who received 15 knights' fees (grants of land) from William the Conqueror in return for fighting for the king personally and providing other men. He provided three knights a month for five months a year to help defend the castle.

Gaol Lane runs from Queen Street to Market Square. It was already called Gaol Lane by 1786, the corporation having bought a house there and converted it into a prison in 1746, following the abandonment of housing prisoners in one of the townwall towers. The gaol in this lane was wrecked by a mob in 1820 but rebuilt and then abandoned in 1834 when the new town prison opened alongside the Maison Dieu. On the old gaol building was an iron rod with four fish that moved when the treadmill was in use.

Gardiner's Lane ran from Biggin Street to Priory Road. This was the original name of Worthington Street as early as James I's reign, but became Worthington Lane around 1800.

Gateway (The) with access off Wellesley Road and Douro Place dominates the modern sea front with its 221 flats and takes the name from Dover being known as the gateway to Europe. It was completed in 1958 built on land between Douro Place and Wellesley Road, following demolition of many war damaged houses.

George Square was at the top of Snargate Street where the bench once stood. On the east side was an opening to the Fish Market and on the west the *George Tavern*. Both tavern and square were presumably named after one of the king Georges.

George Street runs from Shooter's Hill to Erith Street. Dating from 1838, the builder apparently named this street after his foreman, George Fry. All the houses are now post Second World War.

Georgia Way was a path off Roosevelt Road and part of the post Second World War Buckland Housing Estate War. It was demolished in 1965 as part of redevelopment. See Alberta Close for name.

Pier District 1810

Buckland Bridge

Glenfield Road runs from Brookfield Road to Winant Way. There is a Glenfield in Leicestershire, but what was the Dover connection? The road was laid out in 1904 by Major Lawes on part of Old Park, which he owned.

Gloster Ropewalk is off South Military Road, Aycliffe. In Shakespeare's *King Lear* the Duke of Gloster asks, 'Dost thou know Dover?' Building of the railway from Folkestone in 1844 forced ropemaking under Archcliffe to move above Archcliffe. In the 1920s the Borough Council built 100 cottages on the site to help rehouse people from the Pier District whose homes were demolished as part of a slum clearance programme.

Gloster Way is off South Military Road, Aycliffe. See Gloster Ropewalk.

Godwyne Close is off Godwyne Road. This is an access road to blocks of flats built post Second World War on the site of Clark's Nursery. See Godwyne Road.

Godwyne Path is off Monastery Avenue. This is a late 20th century development on the site of the former Castlemount School. See Godwyne Road.

Godwyne Road runs from Maison Dieu Road to Castle Avenue. Godwyne was Earl of Kent in 1057, Governor of Dover Castle and the father of King Harold. The road was laid out in 1870 as part of the Taswell Estate on the medieval Maison Dieu Fields.

Golden Cross Passage ran from St. James's Street to Russell Place. Named after the inn, it was blocked off in 1986.

Goodfellow Way is off Dour Street. Built by the council in 1982, it was named after the first Labour mayor of Dover (1945-49), Arthur Goodfellow.

Gorse Hill Road took its name from the adjacent down called Gorse Hill and became part of Crabble Avenue in 1931.

Goschen Road runs from Astor Avenue to Noah's Ark Road in Tower Hamlets. Built by the council in 1925, it was named after a prominent 19th century Liberal who disagreed with Gladstone over home rule for Ireland and later joined the Conservatives. Following war damage, some prefabs were erected there in 1948.

Granville Street runs from Bridge Street to Beaconsfield Road. The builder, Mr. S. Tucker, originally wanted to call it Barton Street, but, when built in 1882, it was named after Lord Granville, Foreign Secretary and Lord Warden from 1863 to 1888.

Great Street or **Square** was between Bulwark Street and Beach Street. Formerly called Heart's Row, it existed before 1782 and was just a short thoroughfare in the Pier District and was so wide that it was also known as Great Square. It was demolished in 1913.

Green Lane runs from Whitfield Avenue to Melbourne Road. It was adopted in 1982 and runs from the junction with Brookfield Avenue through the Buckland Estate to the town boundary. Presumably its name comes from the green fields that it once passed through.

Grove (The) is a cul-de-sac off Limes Road. Originally called Barton Grove, it was built on the site of Barton Farm between 1900 and 1910.

Grubbin's Lane ran from Bench Street to Adrian Street. Grubbin was apparently the name of the only shop and residence at the end of the street, which already existed in 1754. It was renamed Chapel Lane, since it led from Bench Street to the Baptist (now Unitarian) Chapel in Adrian Street when the chapel was built in 1820.

Guilford Lawn ran from Marine Parade to Liverpool Street. Named after the Guilford family, a Lord Guilford of Waldershare was a member of the Harbour Board for many years, including the 1830s when these dwellings were built on Harbour Board land. Andrew de Guldeford was Constable of Dover Castle and Lord Warden in the 14th century. Sir Edward Guldeford held the same posts in the 16th century and the second Earl of Guilford was Lord Warden from 1779 to 1792.

Hamilton Road is off Noah's Ark Road in Tower Hamlets. Named after the Duke of Hamilton, a prominent Conservative at the time, it was built by the council in 1925.

Hammond Place was part of Liverpool Street and was named after James Hammond, a mayor of Dover and a member of the Harbour Board who died in 1790.

Hardwicke Road is off Maxton Road and is possibly named after the first Earl of Hardwick, Lord Chancellor and son of Philip York, a Dover lawyer in 1790. The family home was a five gabled house in Snargate Street where Maritime House now stands. Alternatively, the road could be named after the architect who restored the Maison Dieu and planned Waterloo Crescent. It was adopted in 1898.

Harold Passage runs from Maison Dieu Road to Laureston Place. This steep footway was named after King Harold in 1862. It was previously a continuation of Dieu (or Dee) Stone Lane and was widened when St. James's New Church was built to give access to the new Taswell Estate.

Harold Street is now in two parts – off Godwyne Road and off Taswell Street. Named after King Harold, son of Godwyn, Earl of Kent, who was killed at the Battle of Hastings, it formed part of the Taswell Estate built by Captain Taswell from 1862 on the old Maison Dieu Fields.

Hart's Row (sometimes spelt Heart's) appears on Eldred's 1641 map and was off Archcliffe Street in the Pier District. Hart is an old Dover name. It was later named Great Street.

Hartley Street ran from Durham Hill to Cowgate Hill. Around 1800 John Hartley owned the meadows adjoining what became Cowgate Cemetery and built Prospect House in Princes Street where he ran a private school for young gentlemen (later housing the Prince of Wales Sea Training School for many years). When the area behind Prospect House was built upon, this road took his name. It was demolished during the 1930s as part of a slum clearance programme.

Hawkesbury Street now only provides a modern concrete spiral access to Channel View Road. By 1798 the old Paradise harbour was a useless swamp. It was drained and built upon, including this street, running from Elizabeth Street to Limekiln Street, which was named after the Lord Warden and Chairman of the Harbour Board from 1806 to 1829, Lord Hawkesbury, who became Lord Liverpool. It was demolished in 1913 as part of a slum clearance programme.

Old Pier houses by Samuel Mackie 1842

Archcliffe Beach by Samuel Mackie 1842

Old Charlton Church by Samuel Mackie 1846

Kingsford's Brewery 1847 painted in 1912 by J. Tucker

Heathfield Avenue runs from Nightingale Road to Park Road. This long road was laid out 1890-1900 by a George Munro and adopted in 1902. George Lewis built 70 cottages there in 1898.

Heights Terrace is off Citadel Crescent, Western Heights. It was built in the 1950s as part of the housing estate for the officers of the Borstal Institution.

Herbert Street is a cul-de-sac off Erith Street. Built around 1840, it was apparently named after the servant of the developer.

Heritage Gardens is off Laureston Place and was built at the end of the 20th century on the site of the former Castlemount School.

Hewitt Road is a cul-de-sac at the junction of Crafford Street and Dour Street. It was built in 1980 and named after the baker's premises that existed on this corner until it was destroyed during the Second World War. This was the family business of Jack Hewitt, a well known 20th century Dovorian, prominent in the Scout and St. John Ambulance movements.

High Street runs from the Maison Dieu to the Tower Hamlets traffic lights. Strictly speaking this is Charlton High Street. It was called Holestreet in 1400 and by 1800 had become Charlton High Road when pleasant houses were built on market gardens on the east side. It was widened in 1899.

Hillside Road runs from Bunker's Hill to Crabble Avenue. An obvious name for this road built in the ten years after Crabble Athletic Ground was laid out and opened in 1897. It was not adopted until1931.

Hirst Close is off Peverell Road, Melbourne Avenue. It was built by the council in the 1960s and named after Hirst Tower in Dover Castle. This, in turn, was named after John de Hirst who was granted Hirst Manor by the Crown in return for a knight's fee (an obligation to provide men to help guard the castle) .

Hobart Crescent is off Napier Road, part of the post Second World War Buckland Housing Estate. See Alberta Close for name.

Hole Street – See High Street.

Hollowood Road is off Poulton Close, part of the Coombe Valley Road industrial estate developed in the second half of the 20th century and named after the wood that previously existed there.

Holmestone Road is off Poulton Close and part of the Coombe Valley Road industrial estate developed in the second half of the 20th century. It was named after the wood on the site.

Horsnaill's Lane is mentioned in the Paving Commissioners' Minutes 1786. One of the Paving Commissioners was a Mr. Horsnaill, member of a prominent Dover family.

Hubert Passage runs from St. James's Street to Castle Hill. Not named after Hubert de Burgh until 1879, it was an ancient steep path to Canons' or Monks' Gate at the castle, known as Monks' or Canons' Path.

Hubert Terrace existed in 1841 and appears at the foot of Castle Hill Road on an 1851 map but was destroyed apparently when Victoria Park was built in 1864. It was presumably named after Hubert de Burgh.

Hudson Close is off Green Lane. Part of the later development of the Buckland Estate, it was adopted in 1982. See Alberta Close for name.

Johannesburg Road is off Melbourne Avenue and part of the post Second World War Buckland Housing Estate. See Alberta Close for name.

John's Place was a cul-de-sac off Trevanion Street containing five dwellings and named after John Trevanion – see Trevanion Street. It was demolished by 1948.

Jubilee Way is the final section of the A2 into the Eastern Docks. This elevated road into the Eastern Docks from the A2 was opened in 1977, the year of Queen Elizabeth's Silver Jubilee. Its construction relieved the town centre of docks traffic until the construction of the A20 through the town in the 1990s brought it all back!

Kember's Lane is mentioned in the Paving Commissioners' Minutes 1786.

Kemp's Lane ran from Strond Street to Limekiln Street and is mentioned in 1778 Paving Commissioner's minutes.

Kentucky Walk was a path between Winant Way and Maine Close and was part of the post Second World War Buckland Housing Estate, but was demolished for redevelopment. See Alberta Close for name.

Kimberley Close is off Durban Crescent and part of the post Second World War Buckland Housing Estate. See Alberta Close for name.

Kimberley Terrace is the name given to 32 houses in Douglas Road built around 1900 and named after the diamond mining area of South Africa, which was in the news at the time.

Kimberley Walk was a path linking Winant Way and Maine Close, part of the post Second World War Buckland Housing Estate, but this path was later demolished for redevelopment.

King Lear's Way provides access off South Military Road to King's Ropewalk - see for name explanation.

King Street runs from the Market Square to Bench Street. Once thought to have been named after Henry VIII who may have stayed in a house in this street, much earlier deeds and charters of the Norman period, however, refer to King's Street and King's Lane, possibly indicating that the Crown owned the area at the time. The narrow street was widened in 1829 by pulling down the west side and setting buildings further back.

King's Head Street in the Pier District was named after the pub in the street thought to have been named after James I. It became Clarence Place later. See Clarence Place.

King's Lane ran from King Street to Mill Lane in an area owned by Norman kings. It was later renamed Fishmonger's Lane.

Cherry Tree Lane 1861 painted in 1912 by J. Tucker

Gate Inn Buckland 1869 painted in 1912 by J. Tucker

Barton Road 1881 painted in 1912 by J. Tucker

Barton Farm 1870 painted in 1912 by J. Tucker

King's Passage This old alley in the Pier District ran from Seven Star Street to Beach Street by the *King's Head Hotel*.

King's Road is off Elms Vale Road and was being laid out at the time of George V and Queen Mary's Silver Jubilee. It was not adopted until 1951.

Kingly Way see Cow Lane.

King's Ropewalk is off King Lear's Way in Aycliffe. Building of the railway from Folkestone in 1844 forced ropemaking under Archcliffe to move above Archcliffe. In the 1920s the Borough Council built 100 cottages on the site to help rehouse people from the Pier District whose homes were demolished as part of a slum clearance programme.

Kitchener Road is off Elms Vale Road. The Monins family held land in the Elms Vale area for centuries. John Henry Monins lived at Ringwould House when several streets were laid out in this area around 1900. General Kitchener, later Earl Kitchener, was his cousin.

Knight's Way runs from London Road to Old Park Hill, Buckland Estate. It was built in 1925. All the streets in the Buckland Estate built before the Second World War take their names from characters in Chaucer's *Canterbury Tales*.

Knights Templars is off Citadel Road, Western Heights. It takes its name from the remains of a Knights Templar church close by, which was discovered in 1806. King John may have met the Papal Legate there. This was part of the housing estate built in the 1950s for officers of the Borstal Institution.

Ladywell joins High Street to Park Place and Park Street. The Well of Our Lady was in this lane and its waters apparently cured sicknesses. 'Pure Ladywell Water' was apparently sold in the streets. The well became the town's first drinking fountain when a pump was added around 1834. A remnant of the well was unearthed in the 1970s. The lane was 14 feet wide in 1839 and little more than a farm track, but it became a cobbled street as part of the development of the Maison Dieu lands. It was widened in 1903 by removing the north side.

Ladywell Place was a cul-de-sac off Park Place. It was demolished in 1938 in order to build the police station. See Ladywell.

Lamb's Lane is mentioned in the Paving Commissioners' Minutes 1786.

Lambton Road is off Coombe Valley Road. Lambton was the family name of the Earls of Durham. John Lambton was Lord Privy Seal in 1828 and was created Earl of Durham in 1833. The road was adopted in 1905 and extended by the council in 1933-34.

Lamper's Lane was off Biggin Street in 1781. See New Street.

Lancaster Road is off Durham Hill. The Durham Hill area was redeveloped after the Second World War with blocks of flats, which were all named after royal dukes, including Lancaster, which gave its name to this road.

Lascelles Road is off the north side of Folkestone Road. It was built in 1901 when part of the lland of the Monins Estate. Lascelles is the family name of Lord Harewood (the 6th Lord

Harewood married Mary, the Princess Royal, daughter of George V). This Lord Harewood was an army general in the First World War, but what was the Dover connection?

Last Lane ran from Queen Street to Adrian Street. Perhaps it should be called Lass Lane since there was a pub there called *The Lass*, which was demolished about 1776. Some think it is named after shoe lasts because of the shoemaking businesses that flourished there from 1710. Yet another theory is that it was the last lane before reaching the medieval town walls. Bavington Jones says that it was once called Bourman's Lane. It now ends at modern York Street.

Laureston Place is off Castle Hill. Mr. Fector built Laureston House here. Either the road and house were named after Laureston where Mr. Fector's wife came from or after her maiden name of Laurie. It is mentioned in the Paving Commissioners' Minutes 1824. The area was previously called Up Market, possibly a corruption of Tup Market where young rams were sold. A tup was apparently a young ram. Until 1801, it was the only road to Deal.

Leighton Road is off Beaconsfield Road. Dating from 1897, it was laid out on part of the Dover cricket field by W. J. Adcock, a builder who was mayor in 1885 and 1890. He chose to name both this and the adjacent Millais Road after painters who died at the time the roads were built. It was adopted in 1931.

Leyburne Road runs from Taswell Street to Godwyne Road. Roger de Leyburne was a Lord Warden during Henry III's reign and his heart is preserved in a heart shrine in Leyburne Church in Kent. The road was originally laid out and built on in 1862 as part of the Taswell Estate by W. Adcock, but has since been redeveloped with new housing.

Limekiln Lane was off Oxenden Street in the Pier district. See Limekiln Street.

Limekiln Street is now a stretch of the modern A20 between the Snargate Street section and the Archcliffe Road stretch. It was previously a continuation of Snargate Street to the old Hawkesbury Street and appears on a map of 1641. Before the street was built limekilns existed at the base of the cliff to burn chalk for lime before being exported. As part of a slum clearance programme its south side was demolished in 1923.

Limes Road is off Barton Road and was built on the site of Barton Farm in 1906. I presume it was named after trees in the area.

Linces (The) is off Roosevelt Road, Buckland Estate. It was built after the Second World War and is one of the few roads on the estate with a local name. Land in this area was called the Linces. Apparently Hlinc in Anglo-Saxon was a ridge or hill and a lynchet was a strip of grassland between cultivated fields.

Lion Court was off Oxenden Street and was probably named after a hostelry. See Oxenden Street.

Lister Close is off St. Radigund's Road. It is named after Charles Lister House (sheltered housing) to which it gives access and was built in 1983. Charles Lister was Mayor of Folkestone 1949-50. His connection with this development may be the Royal British Legion that built it.

Liverpool Court was off Water Lane. See Liverpool Street and Water Lane.

Cannon Street by Tucker in about 1888 *Castle Steet, 1900 painted by Howard Penton*

Pencester Road by Mary Horsley 1893

118

Snargate Street in 1900 by Howard Penton

Liverpool Street ran from Trevanion street to Wellesley Road. Formerly a promenade called Orange Walk and possibly named after William of Orange whose fleet was off Dover in 1688, the street was built in 1817 across what had been a tidal lagoon between two shingle ridges. It gradually silted up and was then filled in. Until Marine Parade was built it enjoyed sea views. It was named after the then Lord Warden and Chairman of the Harbour Board, Lord Liverpool, who was also Prime Minister from 1812 to 1827.

Liverpool Terrace was named after the Prime Minister and Chairman of The Harbour Board and was part of Liverpool Street.

London Road runs from High Street to Crabble Hill. Dating from around 1680, it contained only a few houses until William Kingsford bought the Bartholomew Lands in 1810. It was originally called Buckland Street from Beaconsfield Road. Several fine residences were built between then and 1845. It was the turnpike road to Canterbury and London with the toll gate on Crabble Hill.

Long Wall ran from The Bench to the Old Guard House and was paved in 1781. It evolved from the long wall built on one side of the Pent (later Wellington Dock) by Thomas Digges and was demolished in 1814.

Longfield Road is off Belgrave Road. Built in about 1880, it was adopted in 1898 and was probably named after a meadow that existed there. Further on, behind Maxton and Farthingloe, the hill is known as Long Hill.

Lord Warden Square is at the seaward end of the Viaduct. The *Lord Warden Hotel* was built by the South Eastern Railway Company in 1851 and the road encircling it was named accordingly.

Lorne Road runs from Buckland Avenue to London Road. The Marquis of Lorne was MP for Dover from 1762 to 1766 when he became Baron Sundridge. The lane was so called on an 1850 map. There was a Lorne Villa in London Road before the Lorne Road houses were built on the lane across Brook Ditch meadow in 1897.

Love Lane was named for obvious reasons. Widened between 1883 and 1885, it was renamed Frith Road and Connaught Road.

Lower Row ran from Durham Hill to Bowling Green Lane. Built early in the 19th century, it was part of the slum clearance programme in the 1930s.

Lowther Road runs from South Road to Goschen Road in Tower Hamlets. Built by 1895 and named after a Thanet Conservative MP, it was adopted in 1906.

Luke's Close off Bunker's Hill Avenue was built in 1997 by the Samuel Lewis Housing Trust. It was to be called Preston Close, but this was rejected and Luke's Close was approved in 1994.

Macdonald Road is off Coombe Valley Road. The road was laid out at the beginning of the 20th century and was named after a Boer War general. It was extended by the council in 1933-34.

Magdala Road runs from St. Radigund's Road to Coombe Valley Road. It was laid out on a former brickfield in 1868 soon after the Abyssinian War when General Lord Napier distinguished himself and was given the title of Magdala.

Maine Close is off Winant Way and part of the post Second World War Buckland Housing Estate. Maine Crescent was closed in 1967 for redevelopment and Maine Close replaced it. See Alberta Close for name.

Maine Crescent was off Green Lane and was part of the post Second World War Buckland Housing Estate, but was closed in 1967 for redevelopment. See Alberta Close for name.

Maison Dieu Place is off High Street. Built on part of Wood's Meadow in the 1860s, facing the side of the Victoria Hospital, it took its name from the medieval building close by.

Maison Dieu Road runs from Charlton Green to Woolcomber Street. The road was built through Maison Dieu Fields, part of Maison Dieu Park, which in turn belonged to the Maison Dieu before the Dissolution. Prior to 1862, when it was properly laid out, it was a cart track that led to Barton Farm called either 'Back of Charlton', 'Charlton Back Lane' or 'Back of Barton'. By 1866 it was lined with imposing villas. Philip Stiff constructed 80 houses in 1871.

Malmains Road is off Folkestone Road. It was built around 1900 as part of the Monins Estate. The Malmains family owned many manors in East Kent including Lenacre Court at Whitfield, having originally accompanied William the Conqueror from Normandy. A William de Malmains was buried in St. Radigund's Abbey in 1224.

Malvern Road runs from Folkestone Road to Clarendon Road. Part of Sir William Crundall's Clarendon Estate, it was built 1875-78 and was possibly named after a Conservative politician of the time rather than the town.

Manger's Lane and **Place** are off Crabble Hill. Several Mangers lived in Dover during the 18th century and may have owned property in this area. These streets were adopted in 1974, but already existed by 1850.

Manor Rise runs from Manor Road to Mount Road. Taking its name from Maxton Manor, it was built between the Wars and was adopted in 1958.

Manor Road is off Approach Road. It takes its name from Maxton Manor, which can be traced back to the reign of Henry III when it was held by Sir Stephen Manekyn from the king in return for providing knights' service in the defence of Dover Castle. A Maxton manor house was lived in by the Worthington family in the 19th century and was only demolished after the Second World War. The road was laid out early in the 19th century, adopted in 1922 and extended in 1933.

Maresfield Close is off Mayfield Avenue. It was built in the 1990s. Several roads in this locality take their names from Sussex towns or villages.

Marine Parade forms part of the sea front. Prior to building in 1821, this sea front walk was a waste of shingle with sheds, herring hangs, boat houses and a whitening factory where dogs turned wheels to grind the material.

Marine Place ran from Marine Parade to Liverpool Street. Developed early in the 19th century,

Market Square in 1895 by Fred Kennett

St. James's Street 1965 by Fred Kennet

it fell victim of war damage and post war redevelopment.

Mariners' Court was off Commercial Quay. This was a small opening when the Commercial Quay was lined with properties. Both disappeared after the First World War for dock expansion.

Marjan Close off St. Radigund's Road was built in 1993. Dover is twinned with Split in Croatia and in 1993 the Mayor of Split visited Dover. To repay the compliment of Split naming one of its roads Dover Street, Dover wished to call its new close after Split, but Split Close was not attractive; therefore, it was called Marjan after a hill in Split with cultural significance.

Market Court was off Market Street. It was demolished during the 1930s as part of a slum clearance programme.

Market Lane ran from Market Square to Queen Street. Formerly part of the precincts of St. Martin Le Grand church, it led to the Market Square. A tallow chandler and grocer traded in this lane from at least the 1500s.During the 19th century John Usborne owned the business and took Richard Dickeson into partnership. By the 1850s the firm was known as Dickeson and Wood and by the 1870s Dickeson was the sole owner. His company supplied the entire British army with blanco and had depots all over the country. Dickeson became one of Dover's richest men and founded the Swimming Club, the Rowing Club, the Cycling Club and several other Dover organisations. In 1880 to celebrate the centenary of Sunday School he gave a party for 5,184 children and 1,000 teachers and a commemorative mug for each child.

Market Place and **Square** is between King Street and Cannon Street. St. Martin's Fair was held annually from about 1160 in the grounds of St. Martin Le Grand's Church, but deteriorated into 'riotousness and drunkenness'. Unsuccessful attempts were made in 1743 and 1748 to stop the fair, which ceased eventually in 1847. An open air market was held in the Square until 1988.The present Market Square, previously called Market Place, dates from 1480 when a new Market Cross was erected. Market days were held weekly. From 1605 until 1861 there was a Court Hall or Guildhall in the Market Place with an open ground floor where stall holders operated on market days with a council chamber above supported on grotesquely carved wooden pillars. This was also the site of the town's instruments of punishment: the stocks, cage, whipping post and pillory.

Market Street ran from Market Square to Princes Street. Apparently this road once connected the Market Place with St. Martin's Gate when the town walls existed. On one side of the street was the church of St. Martin Le Grand. Whilst the street name still exists, the area is grass covered with Roman remains below.

Markland Road is off Church Road. Originally called St. Martin's Road when the school was virtually the only building, the name was changed to Markland in about 1906, following housing development, to avoid confusion with other streets using St. Martin's name. It was not adopted until 1938.The Eaton family were prominent Dover merchants in the 18th century. There is a large memorial in St. Mary's Church to Peter Eaton, who died in 1769, which was erected by Mrs. Hannah Markland, his cousin and heir.

Marlborough Road is a cul-de-sac off Reading Road. Built in 1966, it was named either after the Duke of Marlborough or, more probably, after the town of Marlborough.

Marlowe Road is on the Buckland Estate. Several roads on the Buckland Estate completed in the late 1940s were named after British poets and dramatists.

Masons Road is a cul-de-sac off Coombe Valley Road. Adopted in 1961, it first appeared in Dover directories in the 1930s.

Matthew's Place is a cul-de-sac off Bridge Street. One of the streets on the north side of Bridge Street rebuilt in the middle of the 19th century, it was probably named after Alfred Matthews who built many of the houses in Godwyne Road and elsewhere; alternatively, it could have been named after Saint Matthew.

Maxton Road is off Folkestone Road. It takes its name from Maxton Manor. In the 13th century William Archer was Lord of the Manor and the chief master mariner of the 21 Dover master mariners required to supply ships for the King's service as part of the Cinque Ports' obligations. The road was adopted in 1898.

Mayfield Avenue is off Nightingale Road. Part of William Crundall's Barton Estate laid out 1890-1900, it was adopted in 1902. Like adjacent roads, it was named after a place in Sussex.

Mayfield Gardens is a cul-de-sac off Mayfield Avenue. The houses date from 1900 or somewhat earlier, but the road was not adopted until 1963.

Melbourne Avenue is off Green Lane and forms part of the post Second World War Buckland Estate. See Alberta Close for name.

Michigan Crescent was off Winant Way and was part of the post Second World War Buckland Housing Estate. It was closed for redevelopment when houses replaced prefabs. See Alberta Close for name.

Middle Row ran from Blenheim Square to Seven Star Street. It was one of the earlier Pier district streets, existing before 1737. There were three little streets running parallel to each other in the Pier District and this was the middle one. All three disappeared as part of the Pier District improvement scheme after the First World War.

Military Road now runs from Lancaster Road until it becomes North Military Road. It was constructed by the military before 1831 from the old York Street to give access to the fortifications on the Western Heights. Houses were soon built upon it up to the Christ Church schools, built in 1847, as well as side roads such as Union Row, Blucher Street and part of Mount Pleasant. It was adopted in 1893 and conveyed from the War Department to the Corporation in 1955. With the building of the York Street dual carriageway in the 1970s the road was shortened.

Mill Lane runs from Townwall Street to Fishmongers Lane. It was bounded on one side by the old Town Mill, which dated from the 12th century and was rebuilt in 1803, ceased milling in 1899 and was demolished in 1953. Dwellings in the lane were demolished during the 1930s as part of a slum clearance programme.

Millais Road is off Beaconsfield Road. Dating from 1897, it was named by the builder W. J. Adcock after the famous painter and adopted in 1906.

Milton Close and **Milton Road** are both off The Linces, Buckland Estate. Several roads on the estate, completed in the late 1940s, were named after British poets.

Minerva Avenue runs from Barton Road to Mayfield Avenue. Why this avenue, part of William Crundall's Barton Estate laid out 1897-1898, was named after a Roman goddess is a mystery. It was adopted in 1902.

Monastery Avenue is off Godwyne Road. Built in 2002 on part of the Castlemount site, which at one time was occupied by a religious order.

Monins Road is off Elms Vale Road. A John Monins was mayor of Dover in 1372. John Monins was Lieutenant Governor of Dover Castle and held land in the area, some of which in the Elms Vale area remained in the family until developed for housing at the beginning of the 20th century. It was adopted in 1902.

Monk's Way is off Parson's Way, Buckland Estate. Although not built until just after the Second World War, like other streets on the estate built before 1939, it was named after a character in Chaucer's *Canterbury Tales*.

Montreal Close is off Melbourne Avenue and is part of the post Second World War Buckland Housing Estate. It was adopted in 1982. See Alberta Close for name.

Montreal Way was part of the post Second World War Buckland Housing Estate. This path was closed in 1985 for redevelopment. See Alberta Close for name.

Mount Pleasant ran from Military Road to Hartley Street. Filled with very modest houses, this was the highest road across the upland between Cowgate Hill and Military Hill. Before the area was developed at the beginning of the 19th century it provided very pleasant walks and views. It was demolished as part of a slum clearance programme during the 1930s.

Mount Road is off Maxton Road and was adopted in 1959. It was probably named because of the climb to reach it from Folkestone Road.

Mr. Fector's Lane, mentioned in Paving Commissioners' minutes 1783, was behind banker Peter Fector's house in Strond Street.

Museum Lane ran from Queen Street to the Market Place close by the Museum. In the 19th century the fishmarket and shambles were on one side.

Napier Road ran from Auckland Crescent to Hobart Crescent. The obvious, but incorrect, reason for this name is that David Napier was the owner of *Rob Roy*, the first steam vessel on the cross Channel service in 1820. In fact it is named after the New Zealand city devastated by an earthquake in 1931. It was part of the post Second World War Buckland Housing Estate. See Alberta Close for name.

Natal Road is off Melbourne Avenue and is part of the post Second World War Buckland Housing Estate. See Alberta Close for name.

Nevada Lane is off Winant Way and was part of the post Second World War Buckland Housing Estate. This path was closed in 1985 for redevelopment. See Alberta Close for name.

New Bridge is now pedestrianised from Townwall Street to Marine Parade. The actual bridge over the Dour was built in 1800 on the site of the medieval Severus Gate, demolished in 1762, above which was a chamber in the 14th and 15th centuries used by the King's Customer who collected import and export duties. It was probably called 'New' to differentiate it from the old Buggin's Bridge a little further up stream constructed in 1618 from stone taken from the old St. Martin Le Grand. A Custom House was built on the site in Elizabethan times with a platform and battery which became the Three Gun Battery. The new bridge provided a route from Bench Street to the North and Amherst batteries as well as to the Ropewalk on the shingle and Finnis's timber yard where Camden Crescent and Cambridge Terrace were later built. New Bridge was widened for housing in 1836-40. The National Provincial Bank, which in 1842 had taken over Minet and Fector's bank dating from 1686, built their Dover premises here which were occupied later by the Dover Harbour Board before it moved to Waterloo Crescent.

New Hampshire Way was off Winant Way and was part of the post Second World War Buckland Housing Estate. This path was closed in 1985 for redevelopment. See Alberta Close for name.

New Street runs from Biggin Street to York Street. Called Turne-Againe-Lane in a 1540 charter, it was renamed when houses were built upon it around 1785. The Paving Commissioners' minutes describe New Street as 'lately called Lampers Lane'.

New York Rise was part of the post Second World War Buckland Housing Estate. This path was closed in 1985 for redevelopment. See Alberta Close for name.

Newbury Close is off Marlborough Road. It was built in 1966. Both Newbury and Marlborough are towns in Wiltshire.

Nightingale Road runs from Barton Road to Mayfield Avenue. Part of William Crundall's Barton Estate laid out 1890-1900, it was adopted in 1902.

Noah's Ark Road runs from the top of Edred Road, Tower Hamlets. This led to a dairy farm of the same name and was developed by the council in 1931. The farm probably obtained its name because it lay under the hill known as Mount Ararat. Following war damage, prefabs were erected there in 1948.

Norman Street runs from Priory Road to Effingham Street. It was built in 1846 on what was part of the site of the Norman priory of St. Martin. Belgian workmen repaired war-damaged houses in 1946.

North Military Road is a continuation of Military Road to the Western Heights and was built by the military in the 19th century to provide access to the fortifications from the town.

North Road is off South Road, Tower Hamlets. See Tower Hamlets Road. It is on the 1851 map but was not adopted until 1898.

North Street is a cul-de-sac off Longfield Road. This was close to a footpath over the Western Heights at North Bastion and was adopted in 1898.

Northampton Street ran from New Bridge to Commercial Quay. Completed in 1854 and previously known as 'Up the Pent', it was named after the Earl of Northampton, Lord Warden in the time of James I who persuaded James in 1606 to take control of the harbour from the town and set up the forerunner of the Harbour Board. Prior to this road being built it was called Pentside and owners of Snargate Street properties could, at high tide, come out of their gardens and get into a boat. The General Post Office was once in this street as was the Sailors' Bethel and the Wellington Hall, which was a popular public assembly place before the town purchased the Maison Dieu as the town hall. The street was closed in 1950 to provide more quay space.

Northbourne Avenue runs from Astor Avenue to Noah's Ark Road, Tower Hamlets. Named after Lord Northbourne, a prominent Conservative and local landowner, by Sir William Crundall when he planned the road early in the 20th century, it was not built upon until 1925 when the corporation built the Astor Avenue Estate.

Oakvale Close is a cul-de-sac off Chestnut Road built in 1989. The developer of this area was apparently keen on trees for street names.

Odo Road runs from Widred Road to South Road. It was built in 1875 by the British Land Company. Odo, Bishop of Bayeux, was half brother to William the Conqueror. This powerful man was made Earl of Kent and Constable of Dover Castle. See Tower Hamlets Road.

Oil Mill Lane was off Limekiln Street.

Old Bank Lane was probably by Isaac Minet's bank in the Pier District and was still there in 1841.

Old Charlton Road is a continuation of Frith Road up the hill to the Guston boundary.

Old Folkestone Road is a continuation of South Military Road. This was part of an old pack horse track to Folkestone, which became a turnpike road in 1763, but lost its status 20 years later when the new Folkestone Road was opened through Maxton and Farthingloe.

Old Park Avenue runs from London Road, River to Knight's Way and takes its name from the Old Park estate upon which it was built. The old mansion was largely rebuilt by Major R. B. Lawes around 1870. This road was adopted in 1908.

Old Park Hill is a continuation of Brookfield Avenue to the town boundary. Adopted in 1923, it takes its name from the Old Park estate upon which it was built. The old mansion was largely rebuilt by Major R. B. Lawes around 1870. This road was adopted in 1908.

Old Park Road links Crabble Hill to Brookfield Avenue and was adopted in 1908. It takes its name from the Old Park estate upon which it was built. The old mansion was largely rebuilt by Major R. B. Lawes around 1870.

Old Post Office Lane was in the Pier District and was still there in 1841.

Old St. Margaret's Road. See Upper Road.

Ontario Way was part of the post Second World War Buckland Housing Estate. See Alberta Close for name.

Orange Walk is mentioned in the Paving Commissioners' Minutes 1822. See Liverpool Street.

Oregon Path was off Roosevelt Road and was part of the post Second World War Buckland Housing Estate. This path was closed in 1985 for redevelopment. See Alberta Close for name.

Oswald Place is a cul-de-sac off Oswald Road. It was built by William Kingsford in 1871 and named after St. Oswald, King of Northumbria 634-642.

Oswald Road runs from St. Radigund's Road to Bunker's Hill. It was built by William Kingsford in 1871 and named after St. Oswald, King of Northumbria 634-642.

Ottawa Crescent is off Melbourne Avenue and is part of the post Second World War Buckland Housing Estate. See Alberta Close for name.

Ottawa Way was off Ottawa Crescent and was part of the post Second World War Buckland Housing Estate. It was closed in 1978 for redevelopment. See Alberta Close for name.

Over the Wall is included in the 1835 Pier Ward list and in the 1841 census had just one house. No doubt it took its name from being outside the old town walls.

Oxenden Lane was off Oxenden Street. See Oxenden Street.

Oxenden Street ran from Town Station to Harbour Station. Dover Harbour Board leases date from 1813. Built on land formed when the old Paradise Pent in the Pier District was drained, it was named after Sir Henry Oxenden of Broome Park, an energetic member of the Harbour Board for 44 years who directed harbour improvements from 1791 until 1832. It was demolished in 1923 as part of a slum clearance programme.

Paddock (The) is a cul-de-sac off Maison Dieu Road. Houses were built in 1886 in what was the paddock of Brook House, built by William Moxon. The private Dover High School was built on one side and was occupied by the girls of Dover County School from 1905 until 1935.

Palmerston Terrace was in Charlton Green. Named after Lord Palmerston, Prime Minister and 119th Lord Warden, it was built in 1868 facing the river on Charlton Green.

Paper Alley was off Bridge Street. This was the name given to the first houses built on the north side of Bridge Street soon after1828 even though the nearest paper mill was some distance away. The connection may be that William Kingsford owned the land as well as an oilcake mill at Charlton, a flour mill at Buckland (later called Mannering's Mill) and a paper mill opposite. It was later rebuilt and renamed Paul's Place.

Paradise Lane was off Paradise Street. See Paradise Street.

Paradise Pent is mentioned in the Paving Commissioners' Minutes 1822.

Paradise Street ran from Oxenden Street to Round Tower Lane. Dover. There are Dover Harbour Board leases dated 1813. Built on the site of the original Paradise harbour, it was demolished in 1913 as part of a slum clearance programme.

Pardoner's Way runs from Pilgrim's Way to Old Park Hill. Built in 1925, it is one of the post First World War streets on the Buckland Estate that take their names from characters in Chaucer's *Canterbury Tales*.

Parfitt Way is off Mayfield Avenue. It was built in 1995 and named after Keith Parfitt, an archaeologist with the Canterbury Archaeological Trust which in 1994 excavated an Anglo-Saxon cemetery of 200 graves discovered on this site.

Paris Yard was built on land behind the *Paris Hotel* near the Grand Shaft and was later renamed St. John's Place. See St. John's Place.

Parish Yard off Snargate Street appears in an 1875 directory.

Park Avenue runs from Maison Dieu Road to Connaught Road. Part of the Dover Castle Estate, it leads to Connaught Park, which was opened in 1883 by the Duke and Duchess of Connaught. The road dates from 1885.

Park Mews was off Dour Street and appears in an 1898 directory. See Park Street.

Park Place ran from Ladywell to Dour Street and Park Street. See Park Street.

Park Road runs from Brookfield Avenue to Heathfield Avenue. Adopted in 1935, it presumably takes its name from Old Park. See Old Park Road.

Park Street is a continuation of Ladywell to Five Ways. There is an HM Woods and Forests lease dated 1861. It was built in 1863 and was to be called Ladywell by the Corporation, but some of the new residents had already had their properties named as Park Street in their title deeds as the road ran beside the boundary wall of Maison Dieu Park. The residents won.

Parson's Lane is mentioned in Paving Commissioners' minutes 1783.

Parson's Way runs from Pilgrim's Way to Pardoner's Way. It is one of the post WW I streets on the Buckland Estate that take their names from characters in Chaucer's *Canterbury Tales*.

Paul's Place is off Bridge Street. In the parish of Charlton, it was built on land long known as Paul's Corner, possibly named after one of the patron saints of the parish church. A lease exists dated 1820. See Paper Alley.

Paul's Street - see Churchill Street.

Paxton's Lane was in the Pier District and is mentioned in Paving Commissioners' minutes 1783.

Pear Tree Lane ran from Adrian Street to Chapel Place. This used to be a continuation of Five Post Lane into Chapel Place known as Above Wall. Apparently a very fine pear tree hung over the wall of a garden at the corner of the lane in Adrian Street. It was demolished when Adrian Street was redeveloped.

Pencester Road links Maison Dieu Road with Biggin Street. Stephen de Pencester helped Hubert de Burgh defend Dover Castle against the French in 1216 and became Constable of the Castle. He is buried in the church at Penshurst, his country seat. The road was constructed in 1860 and its bridge in 1863 to connect the town centre with the newly developed Maison Dieu Road. Gunman's Mansion was demolished to provide entry to Biggin Street.

Pentside is mentioned in the Paving Commissioners' minutes in 1778 and was a narrow strip on the landward side of the Pent (which became Wellington Dock in 1846) behind Snargate Street, suitable only for pedestrians. It became Commercial Quay in 1834.

Percival Terrace off Winchelsea Road appears in street directories in the early 1900s.

Perth Way is a path off Auckland Crescent and part of the post Second World War Buckland Housing Estate. See Alberta Close for name.

Peter Street. Originally called St. Peter's Street it now runs from High Street to Branch Street. Laid out in 1830 in the parish of Charlton, it was not completely built upon until 1872, according to Bavington Jones. It was named after one of the patron saints of the parish church. The north side of the street was built on part of the site of St. Mary's Poorhouse, which was closed in 1836 when St. Mary's Parish joined the River Union and its new workhouse in Buckland Bottom. The street ran originally from High Street to Maison Dieu Road, but part was demolished in 1959 to allow Dover Engineering Works to expand. Only a short stretch remains, from the High Street into modern Branch Street.

Peverell Road is off Rokesley Road. Built in the mid 1960s, it took its name from one of the towers of Dover Castle. William Peverell, Lord of Wrensted, received 14 knights' fees (grants of land) in return for fighting for the king personally and providing other men. He provided three knights a month for five months a year to help defend the castle.

Phoenix Lane ran from St. James's Street to Dolphin Lane. It was not named until 1879. Presumably it took its name from the adjacent Leney's brewery. It was closed in 1955.

Piddock's Lane ran into Strond Street and is mentioned in Paving Commissioners' minutes 1781.

Pierce's Court was off Last Lane. This was a small offshoot from Last Lane named after the owner. The first Dover playhouse opened here in 1780, but it transferred to Snargate Street in 1790.

Pierce's Lane is mentioned in Paving Commissioners' minutes 1781. This was the name of a local paving contractor and may have been the origin of the name.

Pilgrim's Way is off London Road, River. Built in 1925, it is one of the streets in the Buckland Estate built before the Second World War which all take their names from characters in Chaucer's *Canterbury Tales*.

Pilgrims Place was in St. Radigund's Road. This row of old cottages recognised the many pilgrims who must have passed on their way to St. Radigund's Abbey.

Pilots' Walk, South Pier is mentioned in the Paving Commissioners' Minutes 1797

Pioneer Road is off Crabble Hill. The land was purchased from Mr. Murray Lawes of Old Park by George Solly who laid out the road and according to Terry Sutton said, 'Let's call it Pioneer Road since we pioneered it!'

Plain (The) see Beach Street.

Pleasant Row ran from Durham Hill to Bowling Green Lane. The area was called Mount

Pleasant before it became densely populated in the early 19th century and had a fine view of the bay, castle and surrounding hills. It was demolished during the 1930s as part of a slum clearance programme.

Polhill's Lane near Ship Lane is mentioned in the Paving Commissioners' Minutes 1822.

Portland Place ran from Durham Hill to Cowgate Hill. The *King Alfred* public house was at number 1 in 1800. It was probably named after the third Duke of Portland, a leading Whig politician who became nominal prime minister of a Pitt government in 1807.

Poulton Close is at the top of Coombe Valley Road. This road, adopted in 1973 as part of an industrial estate, is named after the adjoining valley. Poulton was once a parish but now boasts only a farm.

Pretoria Terrace was laid out by Major Lawes soon after the Boer War and named after the town where the Boers surrendered. It was later renamed Brookfield Avenue. See Brookfield Avenue.

Primrose Place is off Primrose Road. See Primrose Road.

Primrose Road is off Coombe Valley Road. It was built in 1865 and named in 1879 after General Primrose who distinguished himself in the Afghan War. The council extended it in 1933-34.

Prince's Street once ran from York Street to Queen Street, but now is a short road from Durham Hill to Cowgate Hill. Considering when it was built, it was possibly named after the Prince Regent.

Prioress Walk is a path from Pilgrim's Way to Shipman's Way, Buckland Estate. All the streets in the Buckland Estate built before the Second World War took their names from characters in Chaucer's *Canterbury Tales*. This was built in 1932.

Priory Gate Road is off Station Approach. It was built soon after the opening in 1871 of Dover College on the old priory site and was adopted in 1896.

Priory Grove is a cul-de-sac off Priory Hill. See Priory Hill.

Priory Hill is off High Street. Several streets leading to or close to the remains of St. Martin's Priory, now Dover College, use the word Priory. Priory Hill dates from 1881.

Priory Place ran from New Street to Priory Street and is mentioned in the Paving Commissioners' Minutes 1822. See Priory Road.

Priory Road runs from Biggin Street to Priory Street. Several streets leading to or close to the remains of St. Martin's Priory, now Dover College, use the word Priory. Previously called Priory Place, Norman Terrace and St. Martin's Terrace, they were renamed Priory Road in 1872.

Priory Steps run from Priory Gate Road to Priory Hill and Priory Hill to Tower Street (also known as Trafalgar Steps).

Priory Street runs from Biggin Street to Priory Road. Priory Street dates from 1783 according to a *Dover Express* article of 1896. See Priory Road.

Prospect Place is at the top of Edgar Road and both were built at the same time. It possibly took the name because of the fine prospect from its position on the hill.

Queen Elizabeth Square was in the Pier District. A Methodist chapel was there in 1795. The square was partly demolished to make way for the railway and became known as '40 feet road' until named in 1878.

Queen Elizabeth Street ran from Crosswall to Holy Trinity Parsonage in the Pier District.

Queen Street Lane ran from Queen Street to Tavenor's Lane and presumably took its name from Queen Street.

Queen Street used to run from King Street to Princes Street, but now ends at York Street (from 1972). It was possibly so named because it was the road taken by Elizabeth I in 1573 on arrival from Folkestone after entering the town via Cow Gate. This was probably the greatest pageantry ever seen in Dover with the tail end of the procession still climbing out of Folkestone when the Queen entered Dover. A thousand distinguished people were on horseback and a thousand wagons were each pulled by six horses.

Queen's Avenue is off Elms Vale Road. The wife of George V, Queen Mary, is commemorated in this name since the couple were celebrating their Silver Jubilee in 1935 when this road and the adjoining King's Road were built. It was adopted in 1951.

Queen's Court was off New Street and was demolished during the 1930s as part of a slum clearance programme.

Queen's Gardens run from Worthington Street to New Street. This area was part of the lands of the Maison Dieu and, following the Dissolution, became Crown property. By Elizabeth I's reign it had become a garden and was probably named after her. Robert Kennet owned the ground in Charles I's reign when he used it as pasture for his sheep, which were then slaughtered and sold in his Biggin Street shop. The Gunmans of Pencester Road owned it and later, George Dell, a surgeon. W.S. Colyer and Richard Winder leased the ground from William Finnis in 1817 and built two rows of houses on it, retaining the original name.

Randolph Road is off Coombe Valley Road. Lord Randolph Churchill, father of Winston, was a prominent Conservative MP and Chancellor of the Exchequer in the 1880s. Sir William Crundall, a Conservative and the developer of this street, named it after him. Following war damage, prefabs were erected in 1948. It was blocked off in 1977. When new houses were built for hospital staff off Coombe Valley Road in the 1990s, the new road was named Randolph Road.

Randolph Gardens see Salisbury Road.

Reading Road is a cul-de-sac off Elms Vale Road. The Marquis of Reading was Lord Warden in 1934 when this road was laid out.

Red Pump Square See Blenheim Square.

Regina Way was off Melbourne Avenue and was part of the post Second World War Buckland Housing Estate. This path was closed in 1985 for redevelopment. See Alberta Close for name.

Reynold's Court see Freeman's Cottages.

Richard's Lane is mentioned in the Paving Commissioners' Minutes 1832.

Rokesley Road is off Melbourne Avenue opposite Archer's Court School. It was built in the 1960s by the council and named after Rokesley Tower in Dover Castle. This was named after the Manor of Roxley near Lenham which was granted to William de Crevequer, Lord of Leeds, by William the Conqueror in return for fighting for the king and providing men to help guard the castle.

Roosevelt Road is off Green Lane, Buckland Estate. It was built after the Second World War and named after the US wartime president.

Round Tower Lane ran from Paradise Street to Oxenden Street. See Round Tower Street for name. Built by 1641, demolition started in 1910 as part of a slum clearance programme.

Round Tower Passage was near Harbour Station. See Round Tower Street.

Round Tower Street ran from Oxenden Street to Harbour Station. It was built by 1737 and ran parallel with the site of John Clarke's pier or sea wall, built with towers in Henry VII's reign. The wall ran from Archcliffe Fort to South Pier Head, making a safe haven for boats that became known as Paradise Pent. The towers are featured in the famous painting depicting Henry VIII embarking for Field of Cloth of Gold in 1520. Part of one of the towers stood as late as 1813. The street was demolished in the late 19th century to make way for the new railway link between the London Chatham and Dover line and the South East Railway line.

Ruffin's Court was off Princes Street. Apparently in this court was a room let to the elite of Dover for private theatricals. It was named after Thomas Ruffin, the builder, who was born in 1705. In addition to building, he sold sheep's trotters and tripe in the town and neighbouring villages. He was also a bell ringer at St. Mary's and a sexton of the nearby St. Martin's burial ground. He was immortalised by Lord Byron who asked Thomas to show him the grave of Churchill, the poet. Ruffin replied, 'He died before my day of sextonship and I had not the digging of his grave'.

Rugby Road connects Manor Road to Folkestone Road. Apparently this short unmade road, containing a few post WWII houses, was so named at the suggestion of a resident from Rugby.

Ruskin Terrace was a path on the Buckland Estate. This is another of the post Second World War streets and paths in 'Poets' Corner'. It was closed in 1985 for redevelopment.

Russell Place ran from Russell Street to Golden Cross Passage. Built in 1838 and named after Lord John Russell, it was closed in 1986.

Russell Street runs from Castle Street to Townwall Street and was built in 1831 when the great Reform Bill was proposed by Lord John Russell who later became Prime Minister. In 1897 it ran from Castle Street to Dolphin Lane only and then became Fector's Place, but now covers the road to Townwall Street.

Rutland Road is off Glenfield Road. This short unadopted road was built at the beginning of the 20th century and was presumably named after the smallest county in England.

Salisbury Road runs from Godwyne Road to Frith Road. Lord Salisbury was Prime Minister three times between 1885 and 1902 and was installed as Lord Warden in 1896. When Dover Castle Estate was laid out by Sir William Crundall this road was named after him. It dates from 1885, but was originally called Ennismore Gardens and Randolph Gardens.

Samson's (or **Sampson's**) **Lane** is mentioned in Paving Commissioners' minutes of 1780. Named after a Captain Samson, it later also became known as Fifteen Post Lane.

Saxon Street is now a cul-de-sac off Effingham Street. A companion street to adjacent Norman Street, it was built in 1846. Belgian workers repaired war damaged houses in 1946.

Selborne Terrace, Clarendon Road. Part of Sir William Crundall's Clarendon Road, he named it after Roundell Palmer QC, Lord Chancellor, who was created Baron Selborne in 1872 when this road was laid out.

Selkirk Road is off Ottawa Crescent, part of the post Second World War Buckland Housing Estate. See Alberta Close for name.

Seven Star Street ran from Council House Street to the *King's Head* public house. One of the earliest Pier streets it existed by 1737 with a public house of the same name. There is a story told that a group of Channel pilots, who lived at one end, suggested calling it Pleiades Street after the group of seven stars familiar to all seamen. Fishermen living at the other end of the street, no doubt thought that this was a bit of a mouthful and decided to call it Seven Star Street. Bavington Jones states that it was previously Fishermen's Row and even earlier Assher Strete. Partly demolished in 1911 it was completed during the 1930s as part of a slum clearance programme.

Shakespeare Road is off Folkestone Road. Built by George Munro in 1897 it was adopted in 1898. Churchill Road, named after the poet and containing Shakespeare Villas was close by as were Milton Villas. Shakespeare was an obvious choice with Shakespeare Cliff just over the hill.

Sheridan Road is off The Linces, Buckland Estate. Several roads on the Buckland Estate completed in the late 1940s were named after British poets or dramatists.

Ship Lane beside the *Ship Hotel* ran from Custom House Quay to Strond Street and is mentioned in the Paving Commissioners' Minutes 1822.

Shipman's Way is off Knight's Way, Buckland Estate. All the roads in the Buckland Estate built before the Second World War take their names from characters in Chaucer's *Canterbury Tales*.

Shooter's Hill runs from Chapel Hill to George Street. Could the same builder from SE London, who named nearby Erith Street, also have built this road and named it after the better known Shooter's Hill? It dates from 1835, but all the houses are now post Second World War.

Shrubbery Cottages are between Dodd's Lane and Manger's Place off Crabble Hill. The cottages probably took their name from R.V. Coleman's house nearby, which was built originally in the 18th century, but rebuilt by Mr. Coleman in 1923. Council houses were built in 1925.

Slip Passage ran from Cambridge Road to Northampton Street and led to the slipway built in 1850 in Wellington Dock where ships were repaired. The slipway was rebuilt in 1952 in a revised position by the Harbour Board, but was closed in 1970 and is now under the De Bradelei Wharf car park.

Snargate over the Sluice is mentioned in the Paving Commissioners' Minutes 1806. See Union Street.

Snargate Street ran from New Bridge, but now starts at the York Street roundabout and runs to Limekiln Street. Mary Horsley's explanation for the name is that it referred to Snar Gate built as part of the town walls in 1370 when the Snar Gate ward of the town already existed. The name may have originated from a snare in the river to trap rubbish before it blocked the river mouth. As the sea receded from the foot of the cliffs the street was extended. The lower part was not developed until after 1606. The seaward side was demolished in 1928-30 for widening and was widened again in 1950, 1972 and in 1991 as part of the new A20.

South Military Road is a continuation of Old Folkestone Road, Aycliffe and climbs up to the Western Heights fortifications to meet North Military Road. It was built once the 1860s military fortifications were completed.

South Pier is one of the pierheads of the old harbour. There were many houses listed on South Pier in the 1841 census, but they were demolished to make way for the railway in 1844.

South Road links Tower Hamlets Road with Noah's Ark Road. It was built in 1865. The Dover Working Men's Institute built the first eight cottages in 1862 as part of an attempt to improve working men's living conditions. See Tower Hamlets Road

Spencer Road was a path from The Linces to Chaucer Crescent, Buckland Estate. Several roads on the Buckland Estate completed in the late 1940s were named after British poets or dramatists.

Spinners Alley was off Biggin Street.

Spring Gardens was off Peter Street. Built in 1830, the name comes from a chalybeate spring yielding similar water to that found in Ladywell. It was demolished in 1959 to allow Dover Engineering Works to expand.

Spring Place ran from Oxenden Street to Strond Lane and dates from at least 1834. It was laid out on the old Paradise Pent in the Pier District on the site of a spring and demolition started in 1910.

Springfield Road is off Barton Road. The name is mentioned in 1901 council minutes. Adopted in1902 it was probably named after one of the four Springfields in Britain, unless there were water springs on the site!

Squire's Way is off Weaver's Way, Buckland Estate. All the streets in the Buckland Estate built before the Second World War take their names from characters in Chaucer's *Canterbury Tales*, and this road, although built in 1948, continued the theme.

St. Alphege Road is a cul-de-sac off Frith Road. St. Alphege became Archbishop of Canterbury in 1006. When Canterbury was sacked by the Danes in 1011 he refused to pay a ransom and was murdered. The road was adopted in 1903, but was constructed earlier probably to serve the new Charlton Church built in the 1890s.

St. Andrews Gardens are off Bunker's Hill, built in 1981 on land formerly part of St. Andrew's vicarage.

St. Andrews Terrace. The name originally applied to the whole of what is now Crabble Avenue, but now only applies to the main terrace of houses. See Crabble Avenue.

St. Bartholomew's Close was built in a chalk pit in 2000 off Tower Street close to the site of St. Bartholomew's Church which was demolished in 1974.

St. Catharine's Place ran from Bridge Street to Brook Street. This saint was an early Christian martyr who gave her name to the Catherine Wheel because she was tortured on a spike wheel before execution. The street was laid out on the site of the old St. Mary's Poor House, which was built in 1795 and closed in 1836 when the new workhouse opened in Buckland Bottom. Comprising just seven dwellings and the *Wheelwrights' Arms* it was demolished in 1959 to allow Dover Engineering Works to expand.

St. David's Avenue is off Old Folkestone Road. The Corporation decided to use the names of the patron saints of England, Scotland, Wales and Ireland for roads on the post Second World War Aycliffe estate.

St. Edmund's Walk runs from Biggin Street to Priory Road. This alley was constructed alongside the 13th century chapel when it was exposed by redevelopment and restored in 1968. It was probably a cemetery chapel of the Maison Dieu.

St. George's Crescent is off St. David's Avenue. The Corporation decided to use the names of the patron saints of England, Scotland, Wales and Ireland for roads on the post Second World War Aycliffe estate.

St. Giles' Close is off St. Giles Road. See St. Giles' Road.

St. Giles' Road is off Old Folkestone Road. The Corporation decided to use the names of the patron saints of England, Scotland, Wales and Ireland for roads on the post Second World War Aycliffe estate. This road should have been St. Andrews, but, to avoid confusion with St. Andrews Terrace, it was called after St. Giles Cathedral in Edinburgh.

St. James's Lane ran from the old Townwall Street to Dolphin Lane. In St. James's parish, it existed in 1641, but suffered bomb damage and all its buildings were demolished after the Second World War. Now it exists only as a service road off Russell Street.

St. James's Passage ran from St. James's Street to Townwall Street. It suffered bomb damage and was demolished after the Second World War. See St. James's Street.

St. James's Place ran from St. James's Street to Dolphin Lane. It suffered bomb damage and was demolished after the Second World War. See St. James's Street.

St. James's Street currently (2009) runs only from Russell Street car park across Woolcomber

Street to Castle Hill Road. Originally leading to (old) St. James's Church from the Market Square, it was built before 1291 and had this name from at least the mid 16th century. Before that it may have been called Broad Street. It was the route taken by the stage coaches to Deal before Castle Street was built and was a fashionable part of Dover with some prestigious shops and business houses, some of which were very old. It was widened in 1896. Run down between the wars, it was badly damaged during the Second World War and, except for three surviving properties at the Woolcomber Street end, it was closed in 1958. The area was converted into a large car park in the 1980s and now awaits redevelopment.

St. John's Place was off Snargate Street. The name could have derived from an ancient Dover parish, which had an altar in old St. Martin Le Grand Church; alternatively, it could be connected with the Order of St. John of Jerusalem and the ruins of a Knights Templar chapel on the Western Heights. Probably, however, it was named after St. John's Mariners Church in the Pier District. It was demolished in 1938 as part of a slum clearance programme.

St. John's Road off Folkestone Road just above Priory Station was built about 1879 on land belonging to Lord Beaumont, a Knight of the Order of St. John of Jerusalem. It was intended to continue the road behind Folkestone Road, but the land was acquired for an ordnance store by the government. It was adopted in 1900.

St. John's Street is mentioned in Paving Commissioners' minutes of 1781 and was almost certainly named after St. John's Mariners' Church in the Pier District

St. Katherines Place was off Bridge Street on an 1850 map and was probably St. Catharine's Place.

St. Lawrence Way was part of the post Second World War Buckland Housing Estate. This path was closed for redevelopment in 1985. See Alberta Close for name.

St. Margaret's Place was off St. James's Street. It existed by 1851 and was built in the stone yard of Mr. Youden, a builder, who was also schoolmaster at St. Margaret's. He gave this row of neat cottages the name of the village.

St. Martin's Close is a cul-de-sac off St. Giles' Road. Having used the names of patron saints for roads on the post Second World War Aycliffe Estate, the patron saint of Dover was added.

St. Martin's Hill. Built near the remains of St. Martin's Priory, this stretch of Folkestone Road between Priory Road and Priory Gate Road was developed in 1843.

St. Martin's Place. Built near the remains of St. Martin's Priory by 1851, it is the stretch of Priory Road between Effingham Crescent and Norman Street.

St. Martin's Street See Effingham Crescent.

St. Martin's Terrace, High Street. Built in 1844 near the remains of St. Martin's Priory, it is the terrace of houses (now shops) in the High Street facing the Maison Dieu.

St. Mary's Passage runs from Cannon Street to Church Street, an old passage beside St. Mary's Church.

St. Patrick's Road is off Old Folkestone Road. The Corporation decided to use the names of the patron saints of England, Scotland, Wales and Ireland for roads on the post Second World War Aycliffe estate.

St. Radigund's Road is off London Road, Buckland. Prior to 1865 the lower part of the present road was called Butcher's Lane. It leads to St. Radigund's Abbey, which was built in 1191 and became a farm following the Dissolution of the Monasteries. Radegund (520-587) was a princess forced to marry Clotaine, who already had four wives. Following the murder of her brother by Clotaine, she fled and founded a nunnery.

St. Radigund's Walk is off Bunkers Hill Avenue. It was built in 1997. See St. Radigund's Road.

St. Richard's Walk runs from Old Folkestone Road to St. David's Avenue. The Corporation used the names of saints for roads and paths built on the post Second World War Aycliffe Estate.

Stanhope Road is off Barton Road. It was part of William Crundall's Barton Estate laid out 1890-1900. Stanhope is a well known Kentish name and the earldom of Stanhope was created in 1718. Captain R. H. Stanhope RN was MP for Dover in 1831. The road was adopted in 1939.

Station Approach provides access to Dover Priory Station off Folkestone Road and was presumably built in 1861 when the station was built.

Stembrook is off Castle Street. It ran originally from Church Place to Castle Street. A large mill at the entrance to this road stemmed the brook, as the river was often called, for many years. However, Stembrook apparently predates the 1790 mill. Before the creation of Castle Street, 1830-1835, and the bridging of the river, carriages crossed the river by way of a ford, which may have 'stemmed' the river. It was in this area in medieval times that the river divided into the East and West brooks. Approved for slum clearance before the Second World War, its houses were demolished afterwards. The road was reconstructed 1950-51 from Castle Street to Stembrook car park.

Stembrook Place was off Stembrook. See Stembrook.

Stone's Passage was between 74 and 78 High Street (i.e. between Maison Dieu Place and Peter Street and contained two dwellings.

Strond Lane ran from Oxenden Street to Elizabeth Street. It was one of the streets developed after 1800 on the site of the original Paradise Harbour and was demolished in 1913 as part of a slum clearance programme.

Strond Street faced the Granville Dock. It is shown as Strande on early maps, meaning beach, dating back to the time when the sea washed the foot of the cliffs. The line of the street was a channel carrying water from the Great Pent to the harbour entrance to help keep the harbour mouth clear of shingle. The street was certainly built by 1737 but part of it was demolished in 1860-61 to make way for the railway line. It was taken over by the Harbour Board, closed to the public in 1966 and its buildings demolished to provide more cargo space on Custom House Quay.

Suffolk Gardens are off Elms Park Gardens in Elms Vale. Adopted in 1965, the developer must have had a soft spot for this county.

Sweeps Alley appears in a Joe Harman list of Dover streets and may be Sweeps Lane.

Sweeps Lane is mentioned in the Paving Commissioners' minutes 1832 and apparently crossed Fector's Place according to Bavington Jones.

Taswell Close is off Taswell Street and was built in 1972. See Taswell Street for its name.

Taswell Street is off Maison Dieu Road and was built on part of the old Maison Dieu Fields, belonging to Captain Taswell, and was laid out in 1862.

Tavenor's Gardens were off Market Lane. In 1642 Samuel Tavenor, grocer, occupied the premises in Market Lane later taken over by Sir Richard Dickeson. Samuel built a small Baptist chapel on one end of his house where he held services and preached. His ground adjoining was used as a burial ground for himself and his congregation. This chapel continued in use until the new chapel was built in Adrian Street in 1820 – now the Unitarian Church. Terry Sutton's explanation is that Captain Samuel Taverner (spelling seems to vary), a captain of the troop under Cromwell, acquired land here, which had formerly belonged to St.Martin Le Grand, and built his house. Converted by the Baptists, he was imprisoned in the castle for his faith, but when released in 1692 obtained approval for his house to be used as a meeting house for the Baptists. Although he died in 1696, the Baptists continued to meet in the house until 1745.

Tavenor's Lane. See Tavenor's Gardens.

Templar Street is off London Road intersecting De Burgh Hill and De Burgh Street. Hubert de Burgh was a member of the Order of Knights Templar that built a church on the Western Heights. Templar Street was built soon after 1863.

Tennessee Vale was part of the post Second World War Buckland Housing Estate, but was later demolished for redevelopment. See Alberta Close for name.

Texas Way was off Roosevelt Road and part of the post Second World War Buckland Housing Estate. It was demolished in 1965 for redevelopment. See Alberta Close for name.

Thomas's Lane is mentioned in the Paving Commissioners' minutes 1780.

Thornton's Lane was off Townwall Street. Providing rear access to some of the premises in Bench Street, in the 19th century it only contained a shop or two and a few cottages. It was originally called Town Wall Lane. Why the name was changed is a mystery, but Terry Sutton suggests that it was possibly named after the first regular minister of St. Mary's Church appointed in 1549, Revd. Monge Thorton.

Tilley's Lane is mentioned in the Paving Commissioners' Minutes 1786.

Tinker's Close. On the sloping ground between the present Laureston Place and Ashen Tree Lane a market was held for centuries to supply the castle garrison. Pedlars and tinkers who frequented the market gave the area its name long after the market ended.

Toronto Close is off Green Lane and part of the post Second World War Buckland Housing Estate. See Alberta Close for name.

Toronto Way was off Melbourne Avenue and was part of the post Second World War Buckland Housing Estate. It was closed in 1985 for redevelopment. See Alberta Close for name.

Tower Hamlets Road runs from High Street/London Road to Astor Avenue. The area was formerly known as Charlton Bottom and in 1800 contained only a few shepherds' huts. A few brickmakers' cottages followed with one or two shops and four beerhouses. The area was called Tower Hamlets by Steriker Finnis, the owner of brickfields there who built a tower on Priory Hill to supply water – a strange name for somewhere with no buildings compared with the East London thickly populated area. The tower still stands as part of a house. It is also suggested, by Joyce Banks, that the area was so named because every Easter for ten days the Tower Hamlets Volunteers were billeted in St. Bartholomew's School for local exercises; however, the school was not built until 1880 long after the area was named. The road was formerly Black Horse Lane, named after the inn on the corner of London Road, but became Tower Hamlets Road in 1866 after the bridge over the new railway line was built. Most of the area was developed between 1846 and 1896 by the British Land Company.

Tower Hamlets Street runs from West Street to South Road. See Tower Hamlets Road.

Tower Hill runs from South to North Road. See Tower Hamlets Road.

Tower Street runs from Tower Hamlets Road to South Road. See Tower Hamlets Road.

Townwall Lane ran from Fishmongers Lane to Townwall Street according to an 1850 map, but an 1872 Ordnance Survey map shows it running from Townwall Street to Woolcomber Street! However, the latter does not appear in Dover directories, presumably because it contained no residences.

Townwall Passage ran from Townwall Street to St. James's Street and was demolished after the Second World War.

Townwall Street now runs from York Street roundabout to Douro Place. The old Townwall Street may have followed fairly closely the line of the old town walls, which were on the seaward side of the road from Snargate Street to Woolcomber Street. The corporation named this ancient street in 1799, but the walls were pulled down in 1818 with no trace left above ground when houses were built. Some of the material was used to build Kearsney Abbey in 1821. Starting originally from Bench Street, the upper part of the street, known as Townwall Lane, changed its name to Clarence Street when Clarence House was built (named after the Duke of Clarence). Thomas Pattenden, the Dover diarist, lived at No.1 Townwall Street which was built in 1779. John Shipdem's Round House was also built in this street, which was realigned and made a dual carriageway in the 1960s and widened in 1992 as part of the A20.

Trafalgar Passage (or **Steps**) run from Priory Hill to Tower Hamlets.The name must commemorate the Battle of Trafalgar of 1805.

Trafalgar Place was at the foot of Priory Hill. This was a row of cottages commemorating the Battle of Trafalgar.

Trevanion Lane ran from Woolcomber Street to Trevanion Street, but was closed in 1959. See Trevanion Street.

Trevanion Place was off Trevanion Street. See Trevanion Street.

Trevanion Street ran from St. James's Street to Liverpool Street and dates from at least 1782. John Trevanion was not a Dovorian, but lived here for many years, became a Freeman and was MP for Dover from 1774 until 1803. He died in 1810. His town house, Trevanion House, was in this area. For 50 years he maintained at his own expense a school for 50 poor boys in Council House Street. The street was closed in 1959 for redevelopment.

Turn-Againe-Lane see New Street.

Turnpike Lane see Dolphin Lane.

Turnstile Alley is mentioned in the Paving Commissioners' Minutes 1786.

Two Brewers Lane in the Pier District was there in 1832, named after a pub of the same name.

Underdown Road runs from Folkestone Road to Longfield Road. Thomas Underdown was mayor in 1731 and 1733. Vincent Underdown was mayor in 1743 and 1745. The road, therefore, may have been named after the family. A simpler explanation is that the road lies under the downs. The road was adopted in two parts in 1898 and 1901.

Union Road ran from London Road to Dover Union Workhouse. So named in 1865, it led to the Union or Workhouse opened in 1836. It was renamed Coombe Valley Road in 1964.

Union Row joined Military Road and Bowling Green Hill. Built around 1830, it was demolished as part of the slum clearance programme after the Second World War.

Union Street ran from Strond Street to the sea front, but now from the A20 to the sea front. Thomas Digges' great dam built in 1583 to form the Pent was built upon during the 17th century and was called originally 'Snargate Street over the sluice'. The name was changed by 1792 when the *Union Hotel* was built on its NW Corner. During the 18th and 19th centuries it was an important street and included Latham's bank and warehouses, the *York Hotel*, the *Dover Castle Hotel* and the *Cumberland Inn*. The Amherst Battery was in the NE corner until it was removed in 1844 as part of harbour enlargement. Arnold Braems, who farmed the harbour revenues in Charles I's time, had warehouses here, used later by Isaac Minet. By 1906 only one warehouse was left. A swing bridge was opened in 1846 by the Duke of Wellington to allow ships to access the new Wellington Dock built in the old Pent and a branch railway line on to the Prince of Wales Pier was laid through the street in 1902 for the convenience of transatlantic liner passengers.

Upper Court was off Finnis's Hill.

Upper Road runs from the Deal Road to the Guston boundary. This was Old St. Margaret's Road.

Upwall see Chapel Street.

Vale View Road is off Elms Vale Road. No doubt a magnificent view was afforded from the top of this road before Elms Vale was built up. It was adopted in two parts in 1896 and 1903.

Vancouver Road runs from Melbourne Avenue to Ottawa Crescent and is part of the post Second World War Buckland Housing Estate.

Viaduct (The) runs from Limekiln Street to Beach Street. The original viaduct was opened in 1923 and was built to provide easier access to the Western Docks. It was replaced in about 1980.

Victoria Cottages containing just three small cottages are off 19 High Street and, when built, were named after the young queen.

Victoria Crescent faces the former Royal Victoria Hospital in High Street and was built in 1838 opposite his grand house by papermaker W. Dickenson shortly after Queen Victoria came to the throne.

Victoria Park is an imposing terrace off Castle Hill and was laid out in 1864 on land formerly known as Stringer's Field.

Victoria Row was off 16 High Street. Containing 14 dwellings, it went all the way from High Street to the river and, when built, was named after the young queen. On the 1851 map it is called Victoria Passage.

Victoria Street runs from Erith Street to Coombe Valley Road and was built in the second half of the 19th century and named after Queen Victoria.

Virginia Walk ran from Boston Rise to Georgia Way and was part of the post Second World War Buckland Housing Estate. This path was demolished for redevelopment in 1965. See Alberta Close for name.

Walker's Court was off Finnis's Hill in the Pier District and was demolished in the 1930s.

Walkers Lane is mentioned in the Paving Commissioners' minutes 1783 and may be Walker's Court.

Wall Passage was an old narrow lane running from St. James's Street to Townwall Street, named after its proximity to the town wall or possibly because its cottages were built from the town walls' stone!

Walton's Lane. Samuel Walton, mayor in 1715, established a timber yard above Paradise Harbour, which was later owned by Robert Finnis and the lane became known as Finnis's Hill.

Walton's Row was a lane leading into Crane Street and is mentioned in the Paving Commissioners' minutes 1781 and may be Walton's Lane - see above.

Washington Close is off Roosevelt Road and is part of the post Second World War Buckland Housing Estate. See Alberta Close for name.

Washington Way was off Roosevelt Road and was part of the post Second World War Buckland Housing Estate. It disappeared in redevelopment later in the 20th century. See Alberta Close for name.

Water Lane connected Elizabeth Street with the old Harbour Station. This little lane was often flooded by harbour water. Water from a fresh water spring was once channelled along the line of the lane and emptied into the tidal dock at the Crosswall.

Waterloo Crescent is on the sea front. Built in 1834 by the Harbour Board on a shingle bank used as ropewalks by a man named Jell, it was named after the famous battle, bearing in mind that the victor, the Duke of Wellington, was Lord Warden and Chairman of the Harbour Board at the time.

Weaver's Way is off Friar's Way. All the streets in the Buckland Estate built before the Second World War take their names from characters in Chaucer's *Canterbury Tales*, and this road, although built just after the Second World War, continued the theme.

Wellesley Terrace and Road runs from Townwall Street to Marine Parade. The Duke of Wellington's name was Arthur Wellesley. The terrace, later named Wellesley Road in 1879, was built in 1846 whilst the Duke was Lord Warden and Chairman of the Harbour Board. The terrace was converted into the Grand Hotel in the 1890s and, following war damage, was demolished in 1949. The site is now occupied by The Gateway.

Wellington Gardens. These old people's homes off Sheridan Road are named after the city in New Zealand rather than the Duke of Wellington. It is part of the post Second World War Buckland Housing Estate. See Alberta Close for name.

Wellington Lane was an alley that ran from Snargate Street to Northampton Street named after the Duke of Wellington. Wellington Passage may have been one and the same.

Wellington Passage joined Snargate and Northampton Streets. *The Wellington Inn* was on a corner. Yet another reminder of the famous Duke of Wellington and his connection with Dover.

Wellington Place is yet another tribute to the Duke of Wellington. It faced Liverpool Terrace.

West Street runs from Tower Street to Tower Hamlets Street and was built in 1865. See Tower Hamlets Road

Westbury Crescent continues Belgrave Road. Built after the Second World War, it took its name from close by Westbury Road.

Westbury Road is at the top of Belgrave Road. The building plots were sold in 1896 and the road was built in 1899. There is a Westbury in Wiltshire, but any connection with Dover is not known.

Western Close is off Citadel Road, Western Heights. Taking its name from the Western Heights where it is situated, it is one of several roads built in the 1950s to provide houses for Borstal Institution officers.

Whinless Road is off Coombe Valley Road. This cul-de-sac, built between the two world wars, takes its name from Whinless Down. Whin is an old name for gorse.

Whitfield Avenue runs from the Buckland Bridge junction. This road, built upon around 1900, soon becomes Green Lane, leading to Whitfield.

Widred Road is a continuation of East Street, Tower Hamlets. Widred was a king of Kent and was responsible for the building of the original St. Martin's Church in 691, which was rebuilt by the Normans. He also strengthened the town's walls and gates of that time. This road was built in 1865. See Tower Hamlets Road.

Wilbraham Place. Described in the 1841 census as 'next to Bench Street,' it also appears on the 1835 Pier Ward list. Nothing else is known.

Willow Walk ran from Buckland Avenue to Brookfield Place. This was a pleasant path, with willows no doubt, that went down to the river's edge behind the houses on the north side of Alfred Road.

Winant Way runs from Green Lane to Old Park Hill. John Winant was US ambassador to Britain during the Second World War and his wife visited Dover in 1942. The road was built as part of the post Second World War Buckland Estate.

Winchelsea Road is off Folkestone Road. Built by Mr. Parker Ayers in 1866, the estate's streets were named after George Finch, Lord Winchelsea, who was Lord Warden of the Cinque Ports during Charles II's reign. It was not so named until 1879.

Winchelsea Street is off Folkestone Road. See Winchelsea Road.

Winchelsea Terrace is off Folkestone Road. See Winchelsea Road.

Winders Row was a row of flint cottages off London Road, Buckland opposite Buckland School.

Winnipeg Close is off Winnipeg Road and was built in 1982 as part of the redevelopment of the post Second World War Buckland Housing Estate. See Alberta Close for name.

Winnipeg Road is off Melbourne Avenue and was built as part of the redevelopment of the post Second World War Buckland Housing Estate. See Alberta Close for name.

Winnipeg Way was part of the post Second World War Buckland Housing Estate. This path was closed in 1985 for redevelopment. See Alberta Close for name.

Wood Street is off High Street and was built on part of Wood's Meadow around 1859.

Wood's Place is off Oswald Road and was built at about the same time as Oswald Road i.e. 1871. The Wood family were landowners in the Buckland and Crabble area in the 18th century. William Wood's home at Crabble Corner was the only residence in Crabble Meadows at that time.

Woolcomber Lane ran from Woolcomber Street to Trevanion Street and was closed in 1959 for redevelopment. See Woolcomber Street.

Woolcomber Street originally ran from St. James's Street to Liverpool Street but now ends at Townwall Street. The street was built on land formed since 1500, but before houses were built – some existed by 1638 – the lower end comprised saltpans. The early properties were occupied by woolcombers and the lane may have previously been known as Blaise Lane, St. Blaise being the patron saint of woolcombers. It was widened in 1855 and 1894. Exhibition Place was built there in 1851 commemorating the Great Exhibition. Its houses were approved for demolition or improvement in 1937 and after the Second World War only two buildings were left standing.

Worthington's Lane and **Street** runs from Biggin Street to York Street. Known as Gardiner's Lane in 1625, it became Worthington's Lane from at least 1786 until it was widened in 1895 by demolishing the south side and then became Worthington Street. The Worthington family occupied premises here at one time as well as owning the *Ship Inn* on Custom House Quay and wine vaults in Snargate Street. A member of the family was a Royal Navy lieutenant who devised plans for improving the harbour in the 1830s. Members of the family were buried in St. Mary's, Buckland and Old St. James's churchyards.

Wycherley Crescent runs from Milton Road to The Linces, Buckland Estate. William Wycherley (1640-1715) was an English dramatist commemorated on that part of the Buckland Estate built soon after the Second World War.

Wyndham Road is off South Road, Tower Hamlets. It was built either by George Lewis in 1894 or in 1896 by William Crundall and was named after the Dover MP and government minister, George Wyndham.

Yeame's Lane was in The Pier and is mentioned in the Paving Commissioners' minutes 1783.

York Place was off Chapel Hill. Built at about the same time as Chapel Hill, it is not known whether it was named after a royal duke or the city of York.

York Street is now the modern dual carriageway from the Townwall Street/Snargate Street roundabout to Folkestone Road roundabout but ran originally from Market Street to Military Road. The original York Street area was known as Black Ditch due to the dirty water running at the foot of the Western Heights. The street was called Priory Lane in 1540, being the route from Biggin Gate to the Priory. Many think the street was renamed after the Yorke family. Philip Yorke (1690-1764) was Town Clerk and Recorder of Dover, became Lord Chancellor and was created Earl of Hardwicke. However, the street apparently contained a row of cottages named York Terrace long before the name was adopted for the street; it is also possible, therefore, that the name derives from the Duke of York, brother of Charles II who was made Lord Warden in 1668 and who later became James II.

Youden's Court is named after the builder and mason who had his yard in St. James's Street. It existed in 1851 but was demolished during the 1930s as part of a slum clearance programme.

Zig Zag Path. Until 1801 this continuation of Laureston Place was the road to the castle and Deal. It was laid out as gardens in 1886, but only a footpath survives. The name is obvious if you have climbed this slope!

Acknowledgements

As always there are a number of people that I must thank most sincerely for their assistance with this book:

Jon Iveson, Mark Frost and Bryan Williams of Dover Museum for their help in making photographs available;

Jon Iveson for his valuable comments on the text and additional information on the history of some streets;

Bob Hollingsbee for once again providing some photographs;

May Jones for her meticulous proofreading and helpful suggestions;

and the staff of A. R. Adams and Sons for their technical assistance.

Prints of the illustrations used in this book supplied by Dover Museum are available via the Museum's website:

www.doverdc.co.uk/museum.aspx

Sources of information

Some Memories of Old Dover by Mary Horsley 1892
History Today Companion to British History
Records of Dover by John Bavington Jones, Dover Express 1920
Dover Express articles 'Bit by Bit' 1904-1906
By the Way – a history of Dover's pubs by Barry Smith
St. Mary's Interior Memorials, Kent Family History Society
Perambulation of Dover by John Bavington Jones, Dover Express, 1907
Research by Terry Sutton
Dover Borough road adoption register
Notes made by Joe Harman
Kent Highways list of extant streets
Ward's street map of Dover
Dover – A History, a Museum booklet, 1982.
History of the Castle, Town and Port of Dover by S.P.H. Statham, Longmans, 1899
Dover: the Historical Geography of the town and port since 1750 by D.R.E. Philpott MA
    Thesis 1965 University of London.
Perambulation of Kent by William Lambarde, 1570
Kelly's Dover Directory 1900
Public Health Act 1848 – a Dover Society Newsletter article by Jean Marsh
Our town, Dover by Derek Leach and Terry Sutton, Riverdale Publications, 2003
Dover Castle, English Heritage, 1990
Research by Joyce Banks
Caring for Dover's Poor by Derek Leach, Riverdale Publications, 2006.
Life and Times of a Dovorian, Lillian Kay by Derek Leach, Riverdale Publications,1999
History of the Town and Port of Dover, Revd. John Lyons, Ledger & Shaw, 1814
1851 Public Health street map
Borough Council Minutes 1901
Dover Priory by C.R. Haines Cambridge University Press 1930
History of Archcliffe Fort by Douglas Welby Polar Bear Press 1991
Dover Harbour, Royal Gateway by Derek Leach Riverdale Publications 2005
Dover's Forgotten Fortress by Janice Welby, Kent County Library
Townwall Street, Dover Excavations 1996 by Keith Parfitt, Barry Corke and John Cotter,
    Canterbury Archaeological Trust Ltd 2006
Dover Paving Commissioners Minutes 1778-1850
Wax, Stone & Iron: Dover's Town Defences in the Late Middle Ages by Dr. Sheila
    Sweetenburgh, Archaeologia Cantiana Volume 124 2004
Various leases etc. held by Dover Museum

Illustrations and their source

Index to Part 1

Bold Italic type denotes illustration

153